rst World War

A SHORT HISTORY OF
THE FIRST WORLD WAR

GORDON KERR

POCKET ESSENTIALS

First published in 2014 by
Pocket Essentials, an imprint of
Oldcastle Books Ltd, P.O.Box 394,
Harpenden, Herts, AL5 1XJ
pocketessentials.com

Editor: Nick Rennison

ISBN
978-1-84344-094-9 (Print)
978-1-84344-095-6 (epub)
978-1-84344-096-3 (Kindle)
978-1-84344-097-0 (PDF)

2 4 6 8 10 9 7 5 3 1

Typeset by Avocet Typeset, Somerton, Somerset
in 12pt Perpetua
Printed and bound in Great Britain by CPI Group (Ltd), Croydon, CR0 4YY

For my grandfather,
Joseph Bloomer (1892–1923);
a victim of the war

'The War was decided in the first twenty days of fighting, and all that happened afterwards consisted in battles which, however formidable and devastating, were but desperate and vain appeals against the decision of Fate.'

Winston Churchill

Contents

Introduction

It was one of the largest wars in history. As many as 70 million military personnel were mobilised, 10 million of them non-Europeans, and 16.5 million people lost their lives in it. It was also fought on a global scale. There had been other wars, of course, in which the conflict had spread across the world. Winston Churchill designated the Seven Years' War 'the first world war'; it was fought, after all, in Europe, North America, South America, Africa, India, and the Philippine Islands. The French Revolutionary Wars spread as far as the Middle East and there were clashes on the oceans of the world, while the Napoleonic Wars were fought in Europe and in other locations around the globe, including the West Indies and North America. The war we have come to know as the First World War or the Great War, as it was often called until the start of World War Two, was genuinely a world war, in the sense that amongst the belligerents were countries from as far away from Europe as Japan, the USA, Canada, Australia and New Zealand and fighting took place in China and on the world's oceans.

This was a different type of war. For the first time, it was a conflict that was not fought purely on the battlefield. It also involved those at home, thousands of miles from the fighting. The concept of total war was invented to describe the new idea of an entire country's economy being directed towards war, factories converted to produce munitions and weapons and people expected to endure terrible hardship as food supplies became increasingly limited. For Britain, the latter was a result of the German submarine campaign that attacked ships bringing supplies from the United States and Canada. On the other side, the extremely effective blockade of Germany by the Royal Navy was aimed at starving the German people into submission.

It was also a war characterised by new ways of fighting. The trench had featured in other conflicts, of course, but never on such a monumental scale, across such vast stretches of territory. For just over four years, men lived in the squalor and dreadful mud of those fortifications, engaged in a terrible stalemate in which thousands died for the gain of a few miles of territory invariably lost shortly after. The scale of the killing was, of course, staggering, a death toll that was made worse by the increasing technological and industrial sophistication of the participants. New and better weaponry was developed, and innovations such as the tank and combat aircraft changed the face of warfare. Old ways of fighting, like the cavalry charge, were consigned to the history books. Mounted soldiers had no answer for barbed wire, machine guns and rapid-fire rifles, and anyway, their use depended on a breakthrough in the enemy lines by infantry troops and that never really happened. The scale of the killing, some would argue, was also a result of callousness on the part of commanders on both sides. 'Lions led by donkeys' is a phrase that has often been used to describe this, the 'lions' being the brave troops and the 'donkeys' being the allegedly incompetent and indifferent officers who sent them to their deaths. It is a view that has been supported over the years by a great deal of popular culture and can be seen in the musical *Oh, What a Lovely War!* or in the hugely popular BBC television comedy *Blackadder Goes Forth*. The work of war poets such as Wilfred Owen and Siegfried Sassoon and the novel *All Quiet on the Western Front* by Erich Maria Remarque, have added to this view. Others argue that these are stereotypes while admitting that mistakes were undoubtedly made – not even British Prime Minister David Lloyd George could forgive the errors of judgement at Passchendaele, for instance.

What was the cause of such a war? There is little doubt that imperialism and nationalism contributed to a situation in which war was the only outcome. So too did the suspicions caused by a series of international alliances that had been created over the decades prior to 1914. In such a tense situation, with Germany and Britain also engaged in an ever-escalating arms race, it was obvious that it would not take much to drive the nations of Europe, and eventually the world, to war. The spark was the assassination of the heir to the Austro-Hungarian throne, Archduke Franz Ferdinand, by a Serbian national. It was all the excuse the Austrians needed to start the war and the nations of Europe quickly fell into line during July and August 1914.

It is vital, of course, that we study the First World War if only to understand how such conflicts start, but it also puts into context much of the twentieth century. The post-war world was a very different place. Frontiers had been re-drawn, nationalities had gained self-determination of a kind and centuries-old dynasties had crumbled. Attitudes, too, had changed. People's experiences during the war, whether those of soldiers on the front or of women who had taken the jobs of absent men, had changed their notions of where they fitted in the world and how they should respond to its challenges. It was a vastly different society that emerged from the war. The changes of that time still resonate now and although it began a hundred years ago, the First World War still has a great deal to teach us about how we live today.

1

The Inevitability of War

...The old lie: Dulce et decorum est
Pro patria mori.
From 'Dulce et Decorum Est', by Wilfred Owen

Death in Sarajevo: 28 June 1914

In 1888, the wily German Chancellor, Otto von Bismarck (1815–98), predicted that, 'One day the great European War will come out of some damned foolish thing in the Balkans', and he was right. Several bullets fired by a young Bosnian Serb radical in Sarajevo were all it took to enflame the suspicions and hatreds that had built up amongst the nations of Europe for many decades.

In 1912, aged 18, Gavrilo Princip (1894–1918) had travelled to Belgrade to continue his education and while in Serbia, he had joined the secret nationalist organisation, Unification or Death, unofficially known as the Black Hand society. For the next two years, most of his spare time was spent with fellow nationalists who sought a union between Bosnia-Herzegovina and Serbia and independence from the Austro-Hungarian Empire.

When it was announced that Archduke Franz Ferdinand (1863–1914), the heir to the throne of the Austro-Hungarian Empire, would be visiting Bosnia-Herzegovina in June 1914, Dragutin Dimitrijević (1876–1917), the chief of the Intelligence Department in the Serbian Army and head of the Black Hand, sent Princip, Nedjelko Čabrinović (1895–1916), Trifko Grabež (1895–1918) and four others to Sarajevo to assassinate the Archduke.

Dimitrijević considered Franz Ferdinand a serious threat to a union between Bosnia-Herzegovina and Serbia, concerned that Ferdinand's plans to grant concessions to the South Slavs would make it more difficult to achieve an independent unified Serbian state.

On Sunday 28 June the Archduke and his wife, Sophie, Duchess of Hohenberg (1868–1914), arrived by train at Sarajevo station from where they were to be taken to a reception hosted by General Oskar Potiorek (1853–1933), Governor of Bosnia-Herzegovina. The Mayor of Sarajevo and the city's Commissioner of Police rode in the first car and in the second, the top rolled back to let the crowd see the royal couple, were the Archduke and his wife, accompanied by Potiorek and the Archduke's bodyguard, Count Franz von Harrach (1870–1934).

Seven members of the Black Hand group were posted along the route, but when one of them threw a bomb that exploded under the car following the royal vehicle, Franz Ferdinand's car sped off to the reception, making it impossible for the conspirators to carry out their plans. The reception went ahead and after it, Franz Ferdinand insisted on being driven to the hospital to visit those who had been injured in the explosion. En route, however, his driver took a wrong turn, driving his Gräf & Stift Double Phaeton car into Franz Josef Street where Gavrilo Princip just happened to be standing on a corner. As the car tried to reverse out of the street, Princip stepped forward, raised his gun and, from a distance of about five feet, fired two shots into the open vehicle, the first bullet hitting the Archduke in his jugular vein, the second striking Archduchess Sophie in the abdomen. The terrified driver immediately slammed his foot down hard on the accelerator and the vehicle sped off in the direction of the Governor's residence. But, it was too late; Sophie was dead on arrival and Franz

Ferdinand succumbed to his wound ten minutes later. During the next four years, as a result of these two deaths, many millions more would die in the horror of the First World War.

The Great Powers

The reasons for the outbreak of the war are a matter of ongoing debate. Each of the powers that took up arms during those terrible four years adhered to the claim that it had done so in the face of aggression by another power or group of powers. There was, however, an inevitability about the progress of events. The alliances that had been formed amongst the various nations meant that by 1914 Europe was made up of what have come to be known as 'armed camps'. Occupying one were Germany and Austria while in the other were France and Russia. In such a volatile situation, it would not take a great deal to light the 'powder keg' of European politics and once conflict was finally threatened, the other nations of Europe fell into line according to their alliances or on whichever side they thought would bring them most benefit in the event of victory.

In 1914, a map of Europe would have looked very different to how it looks today, especially where central and Eastern Europe were concerned. Germany, for instance, covered a much larger expanse than now, extending into areas of modern northern Poland and the Czech Republic. To the south lay the vast territory of Austria-Hungary, incorporating the modern-day nations of Austria, Hungary, Slovenia, Bosnia and Herzegovina, Croatia, the Czech Republic, Slovakia, large parts of Serbia and Romania and some lands that are now part of Italy, Montenegro, Poland and Ukraine. The Russian Empire stretched to the east, within its borders the modern-day states of Finland, Poland, Estonia, Latvia,

Lithuania, Belarus and Ukraine. To the west, the frontiers of Spain, France and Portugal were much the same as they are today, but Great Britain incorporated all of Ireland, north and south.

There were five major European powers in 1914: Great Britain, France, Germany, Russia and Austria-Hungary. Amongst these Great Britain was a superpower with an empire of some 13 million square miles that stretched around the globe and included around 20 per cent of the world's population. The Industrial Revolution had brought unimagined prosperity to Britain and the raw materials for her industries were transported from every corner of the globe, under the protection of the Royal Navy, the world's most powerful fleet. Britain stood alone on the fringes of the Continent. In the late nineteenth century, Great Britain, in the words of Canadian Finance Minister George Eulas Foster (1847–1931), stood 'splendidly isolated in Europe'. This concept of 'splendid isolation' nurtured under the leadership of Conservative Prime Ministers Benjamin Disraeli (1804–1881) and the Marquess of Salisbury (1830–1903), was felt at the time to be the best way to preserve the prevailing balance of power on the continent. Meanwhile, Britain fought to preserve its interests in its colonies and dominions, going to war, for instance, with the Boers of South Africa, an ostensibly unequal contest that damaged Britain's reputation, leading to several European nations, most notably the Germans, expressing sympathy for the Boers. Another war, with France this time, was narrowly averted at the Sudanese town of Fashoda.

France had endured a turbulent few decades. In 1870, the German states, led by Prussia, humiliated her in the Franco-Prussian War that resulted in the loss of the eastern regions of Alsace and Lorraine and the payment of crippling reparations. Victory hastened German unification, with Wilhelm I (r. 1861–88) – King

17

of Prussia – installed as Kaiser (Emperor). The French, traumatised by their crushing defeat, ousted their emperor, Napoleon III (r. 1852–70), nephew of Napoleon I (r. 1804–14, 1815), replacing his empire with the Third Republic. They remained embittered and determined to regain the territories that they had lost to the Germans.

German unification was principally the work of Otto von Bismarck (1815–98), Prime Minister of Prussia. A consummate politician, Bismarck involved Prussia in wars that gave it dominance over Austria and France and persuaded the smaller German states to accept Prussian leadership, with him as the first Chancellor of a united Germany. In 1888, Frederick III (r. 1888), married to Victoria 1840–1901), Princess Royal and daughter of British Queen Victoria (r. 1837–1901), succeeded Wilhelm I, but succumbed to cancer just four months later. The imperial crown passed to Wilhelm II (r. 1888–1918) who in 1890 forced Bismarck to resign and began to pursue policies that would contribute greatly to the outbreak of war in 1914. This 'New Course' as it is known, involved more direct personal rule by Wilhelm and the appointment of Chancellors whom he could control more easily than he could Bismarck.

The austere Emperor Franz-Joseph I (r. 1848–1916) had come to the throne of Austria-Hungary in 1848 and ruled over an unwieldy, multi-racial empire. His time on the throne was plagued by nationalism but he ensured a peaceful reign with the *Ausgleich* – the Austro-Hungarian Compromise – of 1867. With this he created a dual monarchy, making him Emperor of Austria as well as King of Hungary, re-establishing the sovereignty of the Kingdom of Hungary. Franz-Joseph had his share of tragedy in his lifetime. His son, Crown Prince Rudolf (1858–1889) committed suicide in 1889 and his wife, Empress Elizabeth, was assassinated in 1898.

Archduke Franz Ferdinand, victim of Gavrilo Princip's June 1914 attack, was his nephew.

The vast Russian Empire, ruled by Tsar Nicholas II (r. 1894–1917), stretched from Europe in the west to the Pacific Ocean in the east but Nicholas's autocratic rule was under constant threat from revolutionary groups seeking sweeping reforms. The Tsar's position was not helped by his domineering German-born wife, Alexandra Feodorovna (1872–1918) and her scandalous relationship with the unhinged mystic, Rasputin (1869–1916). In 1904, believing an easy victory would make him more popular, Nicholas led Russia into a foolhardy war against Japan, a conflict that ended in humiliation for the Tsar and his people, resulting in strikes, demonstrations and attempted revolutions in 1905 and 1906. To placate the angry Russian people, Nicholas promised to introduce civil liberties. He issued the October Manifesto in 1905, creating the State Duma, an elected assembly that he promised would have legislative and oversight powers, but he remained an autocrat.

Rivalries and Jealousies

In the late nineteenth century, suspicions and jealousies were a feature of the political landscape in Europe. As has already been noted, the French were anxious to redeem themselves and restore their lost territories following their crushing defeat in the Franco-Prussian War. They believed it inevitable that there would be a war by which this could be achieved. The Germans, on the other hand, were not satisfied merely with the acquisition of Alsace and Lorraine. The Kaiser was jealous of British colonial success and the wealth it brought. He looked at the power of the Royal Navy and determined that Germany too must have a powerful maritime force if she was to become a global power. He made his views clear in a 1901 speech at the Elbe regatta: 'We have fought for a place in the sun and won it. Our future is on the water.'

In 1906, Britain stunned the world with the launch of a new class of ironclad battleship. With its range, speed, armoury of heavy-calibre guns – the 'all-big-gun' design – and steam-turbine propulsion, HMS *Dreadnought* rendered all other battleships obsolete. It made such an impression, in fact, that 'dreadnought' became the generic name for such vessels and everything that came before was dubbed 'pre-dreadnought'. The Germans were horrified, describing their own vessels as *fünf-minuten* ships because five minutes was the length of time it was thought they would survive if they were unlucky enough to encounter a British dreadnought.

The launch of the *Dreadnought* initiated a naval arms race between Britain and Germany, each new vessel built being bigger than the last and each demonstrating the latest developments in armament, armour and propulsion. Eventually, 'super-dreadnoughts' were being constructed at vast expense, many of which were still being used several decades later during the Second World War. It had been the Royal Navy's intention to establish a two-to-one ratio of battleships against Germany, but Admiral Alfred von Tirpitz (1849–1930) responded with the building of a powerful German Navy while debate raged in Great Britain about how many dreadnoughts should be built.

Meanwhile, there were problems at the other end of Europe. The Balkans had long been the continent's most troubled region. They had been part of the Ottoman Empire from the sixteenth century until the late nineteenth but by the turn of the century, most of the countries of the region had gained independence. It was an area of great strategic importance and Austria-Hungary and

Russia, which each shared common borders with the former Turkish conquests, had been trying to gain influence there since the decline of the Ottoman Empire. The Russians, of course, shared Slav ethnicity with many of the Balkan nations and, understandably, felt a kinship with them. The German Kaiser naturally supported Austro-Hungarian ambitions in the region and Germany itself had attempted to curry favour with the Turks by promising aid and building a railway between Berlin and Baghdad.

The Slavs, however, had their own ambitions. There was talk of an independent Slav state that would survive without the involvement of the major powers. The chief proponent of this notion was Serbia.

Lighting the 'Powder Keg'

Bismarck had devised a set of alliances that would safeguard Germany against its two principal threats – Russia and France. Initially, Russia had been a member of the League of the Three Emperors with Austria-Hungary and Germany, an agreement that Bismarck hoped would isolate France. That league was not renewed, however, after the 1878 Treaty of Berlin left Russia feeling cheated of the gains made in the Russo-Turkish War of 1877–88. In 1879, Germany signed the Dual Alliance with Austria-Hungary, each signatory agreeing to come to the aid of the other in the event of an attack. Three years later, Italy joined with them to form the Triple Alliance but the Italians were far from wholehearted in their adherence to the agreement, especially in view of the fact that they clandestinely concluded a similar agreement with France shortly after. Furthermore, the Italians insisted that the alliance's undertakings should not be regarded as being directed against the British.

Despite claims by the Kaiser that these alliances were no more than defensive, they gave cause for concern across Europe. The Russians and French realised, of course, that the alliances were directed mainly against them, leading them, in turn, to sign their own alliance in 1894. In 1904, Britain and France signed the Anglo-French Entente or Entente Cordiale, not really a treaty, but a series of agreements aimed at peaceful co-existence. This, in turn, developed into the Triple Entente in 1907, when Russia signed the Anglo-Russian Entente with Britain. Germany now had every right to feel threatened, finding herself with enemies both to the east and west. The peace of Europe looked increasingly fragile with the continent split into these two armed camps and it would not take much to set the European powers at each other's throats.

There were a couple of crises before 1914 that could have brought war. The first occurred in 1905 when Kaiser Wilhelm, on a visit to Morocco, made a provocative speech in support of Moroccan independence from French control. Britain and Russia supported the indignant French. In 1911, tribesmen attacked the Moroccan city of Fez, forcing the French to dispatch troops to restore order. In an act of brinksmanship, the Kaiser sent a gunboat to the Moroccan port of Agadir, ostensibly to protect German interests in the region. When the British again expressed support for France in its actions and began the partial mobilisation of the Royal Navy, the Kaiser was forced to withdraw. Germany was embarrassed and, with Britain considered the source of her embarrassment, anti-British feeling swept across the country. The arms race became even more frenetic.

The second crisis erupted in the Balkans where Bismarck had feared a European war would begin. In 1912, the four states of the Balkan League   Bulgaria, Greece, Montenegro and Serbia –

defeated the Turks and in the following year, Bulgaria, disappointed at the secret division of the spoils from the first war, attacked its allies, Greece and Serbia. The Ottoman Empire and Romania joined in on the side of the Greeks and Serbians and Bulgaria was defeated. The result was a region seething with bitterness, distrust and a desire for revenge.

Countdown to War

The spark that finally brought war was the Archduke's assassination. Following the incident, the Austrians carried out an investigation, but failed to find evidence that linked the Serbian government to the assassin. Nonetheless, there were many in the Austrian government and military who believed that the incident presented them with the perfect excuse to go to war against the nation that was most vocal in support of a Slav state in the Balkans, a state that would undoubtedly present a worrying threat to the empire. It was inconceivable, however, that Austria-Hungary would declare war without German support because Russia would undoubtedly join any conflict on the side of Serbia. The Kaiser was quick to let it be known that Germany would uphold the terms of its treaty with its neighbour and, indeed, German military leaders were also eager to go to war. They were convinced that the time was right, especially as they believed their army to be in a much better state of readiness for conflict than those of Russia and France. The Saxon military attaché in Berlin wrote at the time that the German General Staff 'would be pleased if war were to come about now'. Thus, the Austro-Hungarians were given Germany's full support in moving towards war with Serbia.

The Austro-Hungarians sent an ultimatum – the 'July Ultimatum' – to Belgrade consisting of ten demands, a document that the British First Lord of the Admiralty, Winston Churchill (1874–1965), described as 'the most insolent document of its kind ever devised'. In a letter to his friend Venetia Stanley, British Prime Minister Herbert Asquith (1852–1928) summed up the serious nature of the situation and his perception at the time of his country's position:

> '…the situation is just about as bad as it can possibly be. Austria has sent a bullying and humiliating ultimatum to Serbia, who cannot possibly comply with it, and demanded an answer within forty-eight hours – failing which she will march. This means, almost inevitably, that Russia will come to the scene in defence of Serbia and in defiance of Austria, and if so, it is difficult for Germany and France to refrain from lending a hand to one side or the other. So that we are in measurable, or imaginable, distance of a real Armageddon. Happily, there seems to be no reason why we should be anything more than spectators.'

The ultimatum contained demands such as the suppression of all publications that 'incite hatred and contempt of the Austro-Hungarian Monarchy'; the removal from the Serbian military and civil administration of officers and functionaries whose names the Austro-Hungarian Government would provide and the presence in Serbia of 'representatives of the Austro-Hungarian Government' for the 'suppression of subversive movements'. The Serbs accepted almost all of the ultimatum's points, rejecting the one that allowed Austrian police to operate in Serbia. The Austrians were delighted that the Serbs had not accepted all of the demands and began to prepare for war while Britain and France immediately called for a conference to debate the crisis. At 11 am on 28 July 1914, Austria-Hungary declared war on Serbia, shelling Belgrade the following day. Kaiser Wilhelm sent a telegram to his cousin the Tsar asking for his support for Austria-Hungary against Serbia. The Tsar replied:

> 'I appeal to you to help me. An ignoble war has been declared on a weak country... Soon I shall be overwhelmed by pressure brought upon me... to take extreme measures which will lead to war. To try and avoid such a calamity as a European war, I beg you in the name of our old friendship to do what you can to stop your allies from going too far.'

It was all to no avail, however. On 30 July, the Russian Empire began a partial mobilisation of its forces, at last giving the German military what it had wanted, an opportunity to declare war. When Germany demanded that Russian preparations for war cease, Nicholas ignored the request. Therefore, on 1 August, Germany ordered a general mobilisation and declared war on Russia. That day, France and Belgium mobilised. On 2 August, Germany contacted the Belgian government demanding free passage for her troops through Belgium, a demand that was rejected by the Belgians the following day. That same day, Germany and France declared war on each other and news filtered through to the British government that German troops were already in Luxembourg.

Britain, although in an alliance of sorts with France and Russia, was not duty-bound to go to war with Germany. In fact, opinion was very much divided across the Channel. Some considered the trouble between Serbia and Austria-Hungary to be a long way away and little to do with Britain, a view made clear by a newspaper that sneered: 'We care as little for Belgrade (the capital of Serbia) as Belgrade cares for Manchester'. Others held that Britain was honour-bound to support the members of the Triple Entente. It was all rendered academic, however, by Germany's invasion of neutral Belgium. In 1839, Britain, Germany and the other European powers had been signatories to the London Treaty guaranteeing Belgium's neutrality. On 4 August, German Chancellor Bethmann Hollweg (1856–1921) admitted to the German Reichstag that, indeed, the German invasions of Luxembourg and Belgium were in violation of international law, but, he argued, Germany was 'in a state of necessity and necessity knows no law'. At seven that evening, the British Ambassador in Berlin, Sir Edward Goschen (1847–1924), delivered an ultimatum to Gottlieb von Jagow (1863–1935), the German Foreign Minister, demanding a commitment from the Germans by midnight that they would not further violate Belgian neutrality. When the ultimatum was rejected, Sir Edward demanded a meeting with Chancellor Bethmann Hollweg during which Hollweg expressed surprise that Britain was prepared to go to war over the breach of the treaty guaranteeing Belgian neutrality, a 'scrap of paper' as he described it. This attitude, when it was published, outraged public opinion both in Britain and the United States. At midnight, on the expiry of the ultimatum, Britain declared war on Germany.

The Kaiser is reported to have said, referring to his cousins the Tsar, King George V (r. 1910–36) and their grandmother, Queen Victoria:

'To think that George and Nicky should have played me false! If my grandmother had been alive, she would never have allowed it.'

2

1914
'Home for Christmas'

Shall they return to beatings of great bells
In wild trainloads?
A few, a few, too few for drums and yells,
May creep back, silent, to still village wells
Up half-known roads.
From 'The Send-off', by Wilfred Owen

Mobilisation and Initial Moves

As Europe had hastened towards war, the summer of 1914 had continued as normal. The Kaiser had gone on a sailing holiday in the fjords of Norway; the French President had prepared for a trip to Russia; and King George V had opened a conference on one of the most pressing issues in British politics – home rule for Ireland. Encouraged by governments, however, emotions began to build, leading to demonstrations of patriotic feeling in many of Europe's capitals, including London. British politicians were bullish about the war, declaring that it would be 'over by Christmas', a sentiment seized on by the British people. The German Crown Prince Wilhelm (1882–1951) rejoiced in the prospect of what he described as 'a gay and jolly little war'. Meanwhile, his father, Wilhelm II, famously joked that it would be a case of 'lunch in Paris, dinner in St. Petersburg'. Everywhere, queues formed outside recruitment offices, as men clamoured to become part of what they believed would be a great adventure.

Plans for war had been set in motion many years before. In 1904, the Kaiser had asked Field Marshal Alfred von Schlieffen (1833–1913), Chief of the Imperial German General Staff, to devise a plan that would allow Germany to fight a war on two fronts, against France and Russia. Von Schlieffen calculated that it would take six weeks for the Russians to fully mobilise and transport her troops to the front because of the distances to be covered, the poor state of Russian railways and the inefficiency of Russian bureaucracy. In that time, he reasoned, Germany could defeat France – the plan allowing 42 days for this – before the Russian army had the opportunity to invade East Prussia. The Schlieffen Plan was entirely dependent on German ability to mobilise quickly and invade France before the French were ready to withstand their attack. The Germans would march through Belgium into northern France, 'letting the last man on the right brush the Channel with his sleeve', as von Schlieffen put it. Meanwhile they would maintain a defensive posture on the central and right flanks, in Lorraine, the Vosges and the Moselle. As the army swept down, Paris was not to be taken. Instead, the German troops would pass to the west of the capital, trapping French troops in a pincer movement and isolating the north-east of France. The French, trapped around Paris, would be forced into a decisive battle. Von Schlieffen died in January 1913, his last words reported to have been, 'Remember: keep the right wing very strong'. He was replaced by Helmuth von Moltke (1848–1916) who modified the plan, pulling large numbers of troops away from the main force and using them to bolster the armies in Alsace-Lorraine, at the Russian border and in the east.

On 4 August, German troops entered Belgium. The Belgian army, although only a tenth of the size of the invaders, stoutly defended its fortresses and cities, managing to delay the Germans for a month. Belgian forts at Namur, Liège and Antwerp were destroyed by the Germans' 'Big Bertha' artillery – super-heavy howitzers – but the Belgians persevered in their resistance. The Belgian king even ordered the flooding of parts of the country in order to slow the Germans even more. Nonetheless, by 18 August, German troops had taken the vital fortress at Liège, the city that was key to the control of Belgium's railways. Three German armies consisting of three-quarters of a million men in fifty-two divisions entered the Belgian plains while the Belgians took up defensive positions in their fortresses at Antwerp and Namur. The French commander, General Joseph Joffre (1852–1931) was conducting a counter-offensive across the German border, following the French Plan XVII that aimed to drive the Germans back over the Rhine. It was a disaster, however. On 20 August, at Morhange-Sarrebourg, near Strasbourg, French troops, dressed in their old-fashioned red trousers and blue coats, charged uphill into German machine gun fire. They lost 150 guns and 20,000 prisoners were taken. Joffre attacked again on 21 August, in the Ardennes. Having found the German right and left to be strong, he targeted the centre, but German artillery was more effective in the woods than French weaponry.

Meanwhile, the Schlieffen Plan proceeded. German troops marched for hours through the Belgian capital, Brussels, stories of atrocities – shot civilians and burned villages – following in their wake. On 23 August at Dinant, close to the French border, the Commander of the German Third Army, Max von Hausen (1846–1922), ordered the shooting of 600 men, women and children in the town square. The intention was to crush the spirit of the Belgian people, but such incidents served only to rouse the ire of the watching world and sully the name of Germany.

The Battle of Mons and the Battle of the Marne

Plans had been in place for the creation of a British Expeditionary Force since the Second Boer War (1899–1902) and, according to the Entente Cordiale, the British Army's role in a European war was to send soldiers of an Expeditionary Force consisting of six infantry divisions and five cavalry brigades. The force was under the command of Field Marshal Sir John French (1852–1925) who had distinguished himself commanding the Cavalry Division during the Second Boer War. Unlike the European conscript armies, the BEF consisted of 70,000 regular soldiers and reservists. Although described disparagingly by the German Kaiser as 'a contemptible little army', they were, in fact, a highly trained professional force that made good use of its principal weapon, the Lee-Enfield rifle.

The British troops' first contact with the enemy came at Mons, a Belgian coal-mining town close to the French border. The British gallantly held the line of the Mons-Condé Canal for forty-eight hours against the larger German First Army. Initially, the British were victorious but eventually had to retreat because of the Germans' numerical superiority and also because of the French Fifth Army's retreat that exposed the British right flank to German attack. The battle gave birth to the legend of the 'Angels of Mons', visions of a supernatural force – angels or bowmen – seen in the sky alongside St George, who, some British soldiers claimed, intervened at the decisive moment of the battle. The rumour of spiritual intervention, however, derived from a fictional story written by Arthur Machen (1863–1947).

The Germans recognised that at Mons they had been dealt a stinging blow by the British, as described by German novelist and infantry captain Walter Bloem (1868–1951) in his book *Vormarsch*:

'... the men all chilled to the bone, almost too exhausted to move and with the depressing consciousness of defeat weighing heavily upon them. A bad defeat, there can be no gainsaying it... we had been badly beaten, and by the English – by the English we had so laughed at a few hours before.'

The retreat lasted for more than 250 miles, the British and the French closely followed by the Germans and fighting rearguard actions all the way. At Le Cateau, the British forces stopped and fought in a battle in which heavy losses were inflicted on both sides. Sir John French later relieved the commanding officer, Major-General Horace Smith-Dorrien (1858–1930), of his command for the decision to stand and fight. The German pursuit continued as the BEF strove to delay them long enough to allow the French to re-group and move reserves to the front. Soon, only the River Marne stood between the Germans and Paris.

The Germans' rapid advance had brought problems. As would happen so often in advances by all sides during this war, their lines of communication were now severely stretched, making it difficult to supply their troops at the front. Other difficulties were emerging. In the east, the Russians had mobilised much faster than allowed for in the Schlieffen Plan and were already gaining ground in East Prussia. Troops had to be withdrawn from the Western Front, therefore, and hurried eastwards. Further critical changes were made to the original Schlieffen Plan when General Alexander von Kluck (1846–1934), commander of the German First Army, decided that instead of continuing on past Paris to the west and encircling it, as the plan demanded, he would order his men to wheel in a south-easterly direction in pursuit of the retreating French. It was a major miscalculation, depriving the Germans of the chance to encircle Paris and exposing the right flank of von Kluck's force which was attacked by the French Sixth Army under General Michel-Joseph Maunoury (1847–1923). Meanwhile, in Paris, reservists were assembled and conveyed to the front in taxis. For two weeks a battle raged along a 155-mile front, fought between more than a million troops on the Allied side and almost a million and a half on the German side. Eventually, the Germans were forced to retreat to a new defensive line along the River Aisne to the north-east. It was an immense strategic victory for the Allies, ending what had been a relentless month-long offensive by their enemy. The cost was 220,000 German and 263,000 Allied casualties, of whom 81,700 were fatally wounded. During the remainder of the war, no battle on the Western Front would average as many casualties per day as the Battle of the Marne.

The failure of the Schlieffen Plan ended the careers of several German generals, most notably Helmuth von Moltke. On 25 October, Erich von Falkenhayn (1861–1922) succeeded him as Chief of the German General Staff.

The 'Race to the Sea' and the First Battle of Ypres

The flat, coastal region of Flanders was the next target for the German army and they and the Allies now became engaged in what has become known as the 'Race to the Sea', each side trying to outflank the other and reach the coast. There were a number of battles – the First Battle of the Aisne (13–28 September); the First Battle of Picardy (22–26 September); the Battle of Albert (25–29 September); the First Battle of Artois (27 September–10 October); the Battle of La Bassée (10 October–2 November); the Battle of Messines (12 October–2 November); the Battle of Armentières (13 October–2 November); and the Battle of the Yser (18 October–30 November).

The French Tenth Army began to advance eastwards from

Amiens from 25 September. Meanwhile, the German Sixth Army reached Bapaume a day later and advanced to Thiepval on 27 September, attempting to drive westward to the English Channel and seize control of the vital ports of Dunkirk, Calais and Boulogne. In doing so, they would capture the industrial and agricultural regions of northern France and at the same time cut off the BEF from its vital supply route. Belgium would also be isolated. But during the first six days of October, the German advance was halted by a French force commanded by General Ferdinand Foch (1851–1929) while German cavalry trying to reach the coast through Flanders were also brought to a standstill near Lille. All was now dependent on the BEF holding the coastal strip around the River Yser and the city of Ypres inland from there.

The First Battle of Ypres was the last major battle on the Western Front in 1914. Ypres was of immense strategic importance, both to the Germans and the Allies. For the Allies, it stood in the way of a German advance on the seaports that provided the shortest logistical supply route to Allied forces on the Western Front. It was of strategic importance to the Germans because a collapse of their Ypres front would provide the Allies with access to the flat and easily traversable terrain of Flanders. The Germans would have found it difficult to protect the huge and vital Ghent-Roeselare rail network axis that gave them operational mobility in Belgium as well as in northern France. The German-held ports of Ghent and Ostend would also then be open to capture by the Allies.

Falkenhayn had realised, of course, that the failure of the Schlieffen Plan meant that the war was going to extend beyond Christmas. Britain still reigned supreme on the high seas, given the Kaiser's reluctance to send his ships out into a full-scale engagement with the Royal Navy. Nonetheless, he still wanted to damage British and French military prospects in what remained of 1914. Using both veterans and eager young recruits, he mounted a huge offensive, supported by the powerful artillery that had destroyed the Belgian fortresses. The BEF, heavily outnumbered in both men and equipment, incurred huge losses and was pushed back to the town of Ypres and the 'Ypres Salient'. A salient is, of course, a very dangerous position to defend, surrounded as it is by the enemy on three sides and rendering troops within it extremely vulnerable. Withdrawal was unthinkable, however, as it would send the wrong message to a public at home eagerly awaiting good news. Each side missed opportunities for a decisive victory, the Germans, overestimating the numbers they faced, having abandoned their offensive prematurely. The attack fell mainly on the BEF which fought from a series of inadequate, shallow and waterlogged trenches. They had been nicknamed 'The Old Contemptibles' after the Kaiser's remark about them being 'Britain's contemptible little army' and now suffered heavy casualties as they were driven back towards Ypres. The BEF was decimated and would now have to be replaced by a mass conscripted army along the lines of the armies of Europe. The huge loss of life amongst Falkenhayn's poorly trained student and youth volunteers was too great a burden to bear and the Channel ports remained in Allied hands. The Germans lost 19,530 killed, 83,520 wounded and 31,265 missing; the Belgians lost a third of what remained of their army with 21,562 casualties; the French incurred around 50,000 to 80,000 casualties of all sorts and the BEF lost 7,960 dead, 29,562 wounded and 17,873 missing.

The First Battle of Ypres completed the entrenchments of the 'race to the sea' and marked the beginning of the static western front that would remain in place until 1918.

Trench Warfare

The construction of trenches now began in earnest on each side, resulting in vast areas of interlocking defensive networks that stretched along the 497 miles from the English Channel to the Swiss border. Trenches were not new to warfare. They had been used in the early eighteenth century in the War of the Spanish Succession, during the Peninsular War in 1810 and in other conflicts including the American Civil War. Never, however, had they played such an important role as now and they were employed in Italy and Gallipoli as well as on the Western Front. They have taken on a symbolic quality, forever associated in the collective consciousness with the futility of war and the waste of human life on a grand scale.

Trenches were about 12 feet deep and cut in a zigzag pattern so that troops could find protection from fire from their flanks and in order to stop the spread of a blast along the length of a trench if a shell landed in it. Barbed wire was stretched in front of the line, wiring parties venturing out every night to maintain it and improve its effectiveness. Front-line troops lived in 'dug-outs', rooms used for dormitories and stores dug into the trench-wall facing the enemy while zigzagging trenches ran back to safer areas in which hospitals and stores of supplies were located. Through time, the networks of trenches became increasingly sophisticated. There would be several lines of them running parallel to each other that could be used in the event of retreat. The sides of trenches were packed with sandbags, wooden frames and wire mesh, while duck-boards were put down to provide secure footing as the trenches became extremely muddy and treacherous underfoot when it rained. There were worse things than mud, of course. Rats fed on the dead bodies that lay in the trenches and soldiers often became infested with lice. The space between opposing trenches, known as 'no man's land', varied in width but was typically anything between 100 yards and 300 yards although in the cramped area known as Quinn's Post at Gallipoli opposing trenches were a mere 16 feet apart, leading to the constant tossing of hand grenades. 'Saps' were temporary, unmanned dead-end trenches that were dug out into no man's land, used for listening to the enemy's activities or for mounting surprise attacks.

In reality, a soldier did not spend much time in a front-line trench – from a day to two weeks – before being relieved. It has been estimated that a typical British 'Tommy' would spend 15 per cent of his time on the front line; 10 per cent in the support line; 30 per cent in the reserve line; 20 per cent resting; and 25 per cent on leave, training, in hospital or travelling. A British battalion could be expected to engage in action perhaps a handful of times a year and, indeed, some sectors of the front line saw comparatively little activity at all during the war. Meanwhile, other sectors saw almost continuous fighting, most notably Ypres and the exposed, overlooked salient. Even in quiet sectors there were dangers, however, from snipers, gas attacks, artillery rounds and disease. For example, in the first six months of 1916, the British army was not engaged in any significant actions, but still suffered more than 100,000 casualties. It has been estimated that just 50 per cent of men returned alive and uninjured from the trenches.

The British developed a system of three parallel lines of trenches connected by communications trenches, the front one usually only heavily occupied at dawn or dusk. The support or 'travel' trench was between 70 and 100 yards behind the front trench and it was to that one that troops retreated when the front trench was under bombardment. Between 100 and 300 yards further back was the third reserve trench where troops could assemble prior to a counter-attack in the event that the front trenches were captured. About a mile back there were likely to be more lines of trenches to be occupied in the event of a retreat from the original line. But, as the war progressed and the efficacy of artillery improved, this set-up became obsolete.

The Germans had learned much from the trenches of the Russo-Japanese War of 1904-05, using reinforced concrete to construct deep, shell-proof dug-outs that were ventilated. They were the first to employ the concept of 'defence in depth' in which they would create a front-line zone hundreds of yards deep made up not of a continuous line of trenches but of a series of redoubts from which enfilading fire could cover their neighbouring redoubts. The British would eventually adopt this approach, too.

As 1914 drew to a close, with the opposing armies deep in their trenches, the Western Front was locked in deadly stalemate.

The Eastern Front: the Battle of Tannenberg and the Battle of the Masurian Lakes

Following their crossing of the Danube at the beginning of the war, the Austro-Hungarian forces occupied Belgrade but the offensive was soon in trouble. A Serbian counter-attack liberated the city and drove the Hapsburg troops back across the Danube. It was no better on the Carpathian front where Chief of the Austro-Hungarian General Staff, Count Franz Conrad von Hötzendorf (1852–1925), sent his soldiers forward without ordering fire support or ensuring that his armies maintained a continuous front. Outnumbered by the Russians, they suffered heavy casualties and were soon forced to retreat. In the first weeks of the war the Hapsburg army suffered a third of a million casualties and had a further 100,000 men taken prisoner. Most critical, however, was the loss of a considerable number of junior officers and NCOs who were vital in the complex business of leading what was a multi-ethnic army. These officers had become familiar with the various languages their men spoke and had managed to maintain morale and comradeship. Their replacements were middle-class Austro-Hungarians who viewed the troops they commanded as inferior.

At the outbreak of war, in an effort to bolster his popular support, Tsar Nicholas changed the German-sounding name of St Petersburg to the more Russian Petrograd. Meanwhile, the Tsarina, German by birth, threw herself into hospital work. Nicholas had wanted to assume command of the Russian army personally, but he was persuaded instead to appoint his cousin, the Grand Duke Nicholas Nicholayevich (1856–1929) as commander. Having never previously led an army, he was now put in charge of the largest army ever to take the field. The force under his command faced the Austro-Hungarians and Germans along a front that ran from the Baltic Sea, across East Prussia and Poland – at that time a province of Russia – to Galicia in Austria-Hungary. Endeavouring to gain a swift victory in the west, the Germans did not anticipate much involvement in the east to begin with, relying on the Austro-Hungarians to hold the line against the Russians. As we have seen, however, the speed of the Russian mobilisation and the failure of the Schlieffen Plan soon disabused them of this notion.

In terms of numbers, of course, Russia, with its inexhaustible supply of manpower, had a distinct advantage. Its regular army consisted of 1.4 million troops, with mobilisation adding a further 3.1 million to this number. Although they had the numbers, however, they were ill-equipped and lacked modern weaponry. Against the Austro-Hungarians this did not really hinder them but against the Germans it was a different matter entirely.

At the start of the war, the French appealed to the Russians to launch an offensive in the east that might relieve some of the pressure in the west where the German assault on Belgium and northern France was in full swing. Under Generals Paul von Rennenkampf (1854–1918) – Russian despite the German name – and Alexander Samsonov (1859–1914), the Russian troops enjoyed unexpected early success. This had the desired effect from the French point of view, in that units were moved east from the Western Front to provide support. However, the early successes on the southern front were not matched in the north, in East Prussia. Here the Russians faced the far superior German military command with better-prepared troops and modern weaponry at its disposal. Furthermore, Germany's better transport system allowed their troops to be more mobile.

Russia's difficulties were exacerbated by the appointment of two new German commanders, Generals Paul von Hindenburg (1847–1934) and Erich Ludendorff (1865–1937), who, it was hoped, would bring better strategic leadership in the east. Hindenburg, who would go on to become President of Germany from 1925 until 1934, was the son of a Prussian aristocrat, with a distinguished lineage whose military heritage could be traced back to the thirteenth century. He had retired from the army in 1911, but was recalled in 1914 at the age of 67. The ambitious Ludendorff was from a far humbler background and was almost twenty years younger than Hindenburg. During the course of the next few years, these two would become the real power in Germany in both military and political matters.

Towards the end of August, the Russian First and Second Armies advanced into East Prussia, but the two armies operated independently, one based south of the Masurian Lakes, the other north of them, a far from ideal operational situation. To make matters worse, the Russians broadcast their movements in un-encoded radio messages, providing the enemy listening in with the exact locations of their armies and their plans. The Germans engaged each force separately from the other. At Tannenberg, near Allenstein (now Olsztyn), on 26 August, they cut off the Russian Second Army from supplies and reinforcements. The battle lasted until 30 August by which time the Russian Second Army had been destroyed. Russian prisoners numbered 92,000, while 78,000 were killed or wounded and 350 guns were seized. A mere 10,000 escaped to fight another day. The Germans suffered fewer than 20,000 casualties. Samsonov, the Russian commander, unable to stand the shame, shot himself in the head. The following month, the Germans were again victorious against Rennenkampf's First Army at the Battle of the Masurian Lakes, the Russians this time suffering around 120,000 casualties. The German Eighth Army had won one of the most astonishing victories in military history, destroying the Russian Second Army, giving a severe mauling to the First Army and expelling Russian troops from German soil. These actions, especially Tannenberg, represented a tremendous shot in the arm for German pride. They also established the reputations of Hindenburg and Ludendorff. A lull ensued on the Russo-German front. Nonetheless, there was a price to be paid because the reinforcements that had been dispatched from the Western Front would be sorely missed in the imminent Battle of the Marne.

The War at Sea

As already noted, the struggle for naval supremacy had begun long before the start of the war, but despite the intensive German shipbuilding programme, Britain still ruled the waves. At the start of the war, Britain had 20 dreadnought-type battleships against

Germany's 13; 8 battlecruisers against Germany's 5; 102 cruisers versus Germany's 41; 301 destroyers against Germany's 144; and 78 submarines against Germany's 30. The British Grand Fleet was based at Scapa Flow in the Orkney Islands although other naval bases such as Chatham, Portsmouth, Plymouth and Rosyth were also used. The German High Seas Fleet was distributed amongst the ports of Bremen, Emden, Wilhelmshaven, Kiel and Cuxhaven. There were also vessels of both sides patrolling the oceans of the world. During the war, however, there was little contact between the opposing navies. One reason was the importance of the Royal Navy to the British war effort. In fact, Winston Churchill famously described British naval Commander-in-Chief, Admiral John Jellicoe (1859–1935), as 'the only man on either side who could lose the war in an afternoon'.

The first real naval action of the war occurred in August 1914 at Heligoland Bight off the German coast where the British planned to intercept German destroyers on their daily patrols. A force of thirty-one destroyers and two cruisers, commanded by Commodore Reginald Tyrwhitt (1870–1951) and submarines under the command of Commodore Roger Keyes (1872–1945) was dispatched to confront the enemy vessels, supported by six light cruisers and five battlecruisers. The action proved highly successful for the British. Three German light cruisers and a destroyer were sunk while another three light cruisers were damaged. The German losses were 712 killed, 530 injured and 336 taken prisoner. The British suffered some damage to 4 vessels, 35 dead and 40 wounded. The victorious British ships were welcomed home by cheering crowds but the battle resulted in the decision by the German government and, in particular, the Kaiser, to restrict further engagement with the enemy by ordering the German fleet to remain in port. This enabled Britain to maintain a blockade of German ports, restricting access to trade and imports of vital supplies. The only actions that the German navy was allowed to mount were hit-and-run raids on ports on the British east coast, such as the bombardment of Yarmouth and Lowestoft. In Lowestoft, 200 houses and 2 gun batteries were destroyed, 3 people were killed and 12 were injured. The objective of such engagements was to lure British ships out of port where they would find themselves in conditions better suited to the Germans.

The next major naval engagement was fought at Dogger Bank in the North Sea on 24 January 1915. The Royal Navy was already at an advantage, having been passed German codebooks obtained by the Russians. This enabled them to intercept coded messages detailing the whereabouts of a German raiding squadron. The British ships found it exactly where it was supposed to be, at Dogger Bank, but the smaller and slower German force made a run for it, the British in hot pursuit. Engaging them with long-range gunfire, the British succeeded in sinking the German cruiser, the *Blücher*, with the loss of 954 lives. The remainder of the German squadron made it safely back to harbour.

Naval action was not limited to the North Sea, however. British merchant shipping was at the mercy of German surface raiders across the world's oceans. Vessels such as the SMS *Emden*, the SMS *Dresden* and the SMS *Karlsruhe* not only sank Allied ships, they also mounted raids on shore installations and bases. German Vice-Admiral Maximilian von Spee (1861–1914) commanded a naval squadron that had been based at Tsingtao within the German concession on the coast of China, but was forced to put to sea when the base was overrun by Japanese forces in 1914. After that, he led his ships on raids on Allied shipping and bases across the Pacific. On 1 November 1914, his ships sank two British armoured cruisers – HMS *Good Hope* and HMS *Monmouth* – under Rear-Admiral Sir Christopher Craddock (1862–1914) off the Chilean coast in the Battle of Coronel. The British lost 1,570 men, the Germans just 3. It was the Royal Navy's first defeat since the Battle of Lake Champlain in the War of 1812 and there was an immediate call for revenge back in London. A large naval force, assembled under the command of Vice-Admiral Sir Doveton Sturdee (1859–1925), won a major victory against von Spee's squadron in the Battle of the Falkland Islands, only one German vessel managing to escape. Von Spee and his two sons drowned in the battle along with 2,000 other German sailors. Meanwhile, the German raider, the SMS *Königsberg*, operating in the Indian Ocean and attacking British shipping making for the Suez Canal, was cornered and forced to scuttle in the mouth of the River Rufiji in German East Africa. She had sunk HMS *City of Winchester*, consigning to the ocean floor most of Ceylon's 1914 tea crop, and had also delayed the first ships carrying Australian and New Zealand troops to the battlefields of Europe.

The most famous of the German raiders was the remarkable light cruiser, *Emden*. She was captained by the impressive Karl von Müller (1873–1923) who was given free rein by German command to raid independently in the Indian Ocean. In two months, *Emden*, cleverly disguised with a dummy funnel to resemble a British warship, sank nearly two dozen ships. She also bombarded Madras, destroying 50,000 tonnes of petroleum and at Penang sank a Russian cruiser and a French destroyer. She was eventually sunk in the Cook Islands by the more powerful Australian cruiser, HMAS *Sydney*. Von Müller surrendered but some of his crew, led by First Lieutenant Hellmuth von Mücke (1881–1957), managed to escape and in one of the greatest adventures of the war journeyed to the Dutch East Indies and

Yemen before travelling to Constantinople and finally making it back to Germany.

A World War

The British declaration of war on Germany and its allies also committed her colonies and dominions to war and more than 2.5 million men would fight in the armies of the dominions as well as many thousands of volunteers from the Crown colonies. On 6 August 1914, therefore, two days after declaring war on Germany, Britain sent telegrams to the governments of Australia, New Zealand and South Africa requesting that they seize all nearby German colonies. A telegram was also sent to British ally Japan asking her to attack all German merchant shipping. Australia and New Zealand immediately set about the capture of all German garrisons in the vicinity. New Zealand took Samoa, while Australian troops captured German New Guinea, Papua and the islands that formed the Bismarck Archipelago, bringing an end to the German Empire in the southern Pacific for the loss of six Australians and no New Zealanders.

In the north Pacific on 12 August, the British China Squadron attacked and destroyed a German radio station on the island of Yap. Meanwhile, Japan, with her own expansionist ambitions in the Pacific, declared war on Germany on 23 August and began to seize all the remaining German possessions in the northern Pacific, including the Marshall, Caroline and Marianas Islands. Japan next struck the strategically important but heavily fortified German naval base at Tsingtao (modern-day Qingdao) on the coast of the Chinese mainland. Japanese ships imposed a blockade and assembled an invading force of 50,000 men that included one and a half battalions of British troops. Tsingtao fell on 7 November,

Japan suffering 6,000 casualties, the Germans 600. This brought the German Empire in the Pacific to an end.

Like every other major power, Germany had taken part in the 'Scramble for Africa' in the nineteenth century. Her colonies, all of which shared borders with British and French colonies, included Togo, the Cameroons, German South-West Africa (now Namibia) and German East Africa (now Tanzania). The British colony of South Africa had a large Afrikaner population, many of whom sympathised with Germany rather than Britain. They rebelled when Britain appealed to South Africa for help at the outbreak of war, but their revolt was quashed by armies led by the prominent South African statesmen, Louis Botha (1862–1919) and Jan Smuts (1870–1950), who then set about capturing the nearby colony of German South-West Africa. The retreating and heavily outnumbered German garrison quickly surrendered, the territory finally falling to the South Africans on 9 July 1915 for the loss of only 500 men.

For the Allies the war in West Africa started well. Togoland fell in just three weeks but Cameroon proved more difficult. The German garrison there, supplemented by indigenous troops, was well equipped and well disciplined. They had machine guns and light artillery and were able to operate in mountainous jungle country. Most importantly, however, they had a superb commander, Colonel Carl Zimmerman. Fighting a series of running battles, Zimmerman was never defeated, eluding his pursuers until February 1916 when he led his troops into neutral Spanish territory.

Meanwhile, in German South-East Africa, the British faced another German commander of genius, Colonel Paul von Lettow-Vorbeck (1870–1964). Invading from Kenya, the British were twice defeated in battle by his troops. Eventually, he abandoned conventional warfare and adopted guerrilla tactics, the ensuing campaign being described by one commentator as 'the greatest single guerrilla operation in history, and the most successful'. His extraordinarily mobile force made good use of indigenous troops with local knowledge and he made life very difficult for Allied commanders, including Jan Smuts who had himself spearheaded a very successful guerrilla campaign during the Second Boer War. Lettow-Vorbeck would lead the Allies a merry dance until 1918 when he was driven from South-East Africa by sheer weight of numbers. He simply invaded Mozambique and then re-entered South-East Africa from where he launched an invasion of Northern Rhodesia (now Zimbabwe). When the war ended in 1918, he was the last German commander to surrender to the British.

The Home Front

The Prime Minister of the United Kingdom in 1914 was Herbert Henry Asquith, leading a Liberal government that had been in power since 1905, with Asquith as Prime Minister since 1908. The main political issue of the day was the situation in Ireland but there was also industrial unrest and the increasingly violent acts of the suffragettes to be dealt with. These issues were consigned to the shadows by the approach of war. There was a fear of invasion about which the Committee of Imperial Defence – the government body charged with organising Britain's defence and military preparations – had written numerous papers since its establishment in 1904. As the atmosphere in the country grew tense and antipathy towards Germans intensified, the government introduced the Defence of the Realm Act 1914 (DORA) that substantially increased the power of the state to control and act against what were described as 'unpatriotic' forces. 'No person shall by word of mouth or in writing spread reports likely to cause disaffection or alarm among any of His Majesty's forces or among the civilian population' read one section and, indeed, a number of anti-war activists such as Willie Gallacher (1881–1965), John William Muir (1879–1931), Bertrand Russell (1872–1970), John Maclean (1879–1923) and James Maxton (1885–1946) were amongst those imprisoned under the act. Germans and Austrians residing in Britain were categorised as 'enemy aliens' and were interned, deported or had restrictions placed upon them visiting particular parts of the country. Censorship of the post and the press was introduced; the press could not report troop movements, numbers or operational activity of any kind that would be useful to the enemy. The penalty for breaching these regulations with the intention of helping the enemy was death and ten people were executed for such infractions.

Many seemingly innocent activities became prohibited, including kite-flying, feeding bread to wild animals, starting bonfires and the purchase and consumption of alcohol was restricted. Indeed, alcoholic drinks began to be watered down and the opening times of pubs were restricted for the first time, to between noon and 3pm and from 6.30 to 9.30pm.

In Germany, meanwhile, it has often been said that the outbreak of war was greeted with euphoria, but the reality was almost certainly more complex than that. Certainly there was pride that all the parties in the Reichstag – Germany's parliament – including the Social Democrats who had until then been anti-militaristic, unanimously voted for war. It was hoped that Germany's decades of internal political strife were now at an end. When the German army recorded a string of victories in the early days of the war, the feeling of what could be achieved by a unified Germany was reinforced. The feeling of the time has been described as the 'Spirit

47

of 1914' and is demonstrated by the estimated one million war poems that were sent to Germany's national newspapers during August. Meanwhile, countless leaflets and newspaper editorials hailed the political unity that war had engendered. However, there was also considerable apprehension about the conflict, especially as families watched their sons and husbands march off to war but it was subsumed by the hope that political unity was a reality and by the desire not to undermine the support of the troops heading for the front. On the other hand, while the German army may have been prepared for war, the German economy was not and this would be a recurring feature of the German war effort. The British blockade of German ports was devastating as Germany imported a substantial part of its food and raw materials by sea.

The War in the Air

Man had taken to the air in balloons as early as 1783 when the Montgolfier brothers had carried out their first experiments and Étienne Montgolfier (1745–1799) had undertaken the first manned ascent. Since then, many had tried to devise a means of controlling the speed and direction of balloons and render them capable of being much more than a sideshow attraction. In 1894, the German Count Ferdinand von Zeppelin patented a design for a cigar-shaped airship consisting of flexibly articulated rigid sections, the front section carrying the crew and the craft's engines. In 1900, he began using a petrol engine to drive the airship. A fleet of Zeppelins, as they were called, was soon providing the first passenger air service. Then, in 1903, the Wright Brothers made the first flight in a heavier-than-air machine, and six years later the Frenchman Louis Blériot (1872–1936) made the first powered flight across the English Channel. Soon after, aircraft of all sorts – monoplanes, biplanes and triplanes – were rolling out of factories in Europe, America and Britain and, of course, their possibilities for use in war were being analysed by military minds anticipating a European war in the next few years.

Tethered observation balloons had been used in the French Revolutionary Wars, in the American Civil War and during the Franco-Prussian War. They came into their own, however, in the First World War. The British were initially behind in their technology, using spherical balloons but they quickly replaced these with balloons of French and Italian design that could be flown and could operate in bad weather. These balloons allowed the artillery on the ground to be targeted more accurately, a balloon-borne observer able to see more than one based on the ground. They were strategically vital and were heavily protected by anti-aircraft guns and eventually by fighter aircraft. Their crews were the first to utilise the parachute, albeit in a primitive form. Germany, meanwhile, used Zeppelin airships for reconnaissance over the North Sea and for bombing raids such as those at Great Yarmouth and London in 1915. By 1916, Zeppelins were around 660 feet in length, could carry loads of three to four tons of bombs and could fly at speeds between 61 and 82 miles per hour. They were developed to fly higher, at altitudes up to 24,900 feet, and further. LZ104, for instance, flew from Yambol in Bulgaria to German East Africa (modern-day Tanzania) to supply German troops there, a distance of 4,199 miles that it covered in 95 hours.

At the outbreak of hostilities, there was considerable debate about the use of aircraft in war. It was soon realised, however, that they could be effective in a reconnaissance role. In one particular instance, on 22 August 1914, the crew of a British reconnaissance plane was able to report to British High Command that the German General Alexander von Kluck's army was making preparations to surround the British Expeditionary Force. Although it contradicted all other intelligence, the commanders took it seriously and were able to order a withdrawal towards Mons, probably saving the lives of around 100,000 soldiers. Again in 1914, French planes warned of the change in direction made by the German army that allowed the Allied counter-attack on the Marne.

To begin with, however, the number of aircraft available was small. The Germans, relying mainly on Zeppelins, had about 230 serviceable aircraft, the French had 138 while the British had about 63, mostly two-seaters that could attain a speed of 62 miles per hour and reach an altitude of just over 3,000 feet. The British planes were flown by members of the Royal Flying Corps (RFC) – the air battalion of the Royal Engineers – and the Royal Naval Air Service. Pilots were generally members of the upper class who regarded flying as a hobby and the planes were manufactured at the Royal Aircraft Factory at Farnborough or by the private companies Sopwith Aviation or de Havilland.

Even while observing, or photographing the enemy lines, aircraft crew were armed with rifles and revolvers and they often came under intense fire from the ground. In the first few months of 1915, however, planes were increasingly used in an offensive role, strafing enemy trenches with machine guns and dropping bombs on roads, railway lines and ammunition stores. Their comrades on the ground did not always welcome them as their activities often stirred up enemy activity. There was also resentment that aircrews could return to base far behind the lines and spend their evenings relaxing far from danger. Soldiers were also suspicious about the astonishing camaraderie that existed between pilots of both sides. Before long, however, this camaraderie was tested when skirmishing and dogfights became the norm in the skies of the Western Front. Planes would fly in a V-formation until contact was made with enemy planes, at which point they would break up and fight individually. Manoeuvrability and speed were essential in the aircraft and tactics such as attacking with the sun behind were employed. Pilots showed extraordinary skill and courage. The British did not even have parachutes, considering them to be 'un-British'. The Germans did have them and their survival rate was considerably higher than that of the British, particularly as they rarely flew beyond their own front line. In fact, at one point in the war, the life expectancy of a British pilot was little more than a couple of weeks and, by 1917, 50 British planes were being lost every week. The Lewis gun was soon adapted to fit British aircraft, being fixed to the side. There was the constant danger of a propeller being shot off by a plane's own bullets until the Dutchman, Anthony Fokker, invented an interruptible gear for the Germans. It prevented the machine gun from firing when the blade of a propeller passed in front of it.

At the start of the war, Allied aircraft such as the British DH.2 and the French SPAD were fairly successful, but the 1915 introduction by the Germans of the Fokker Eindecker with Fokker's interruptive gear swung the advantage to them. The development in 1916 of the French Nieuport XVII and the British two-seater biplane the Airco DH.4, designed by Geoffrey de Havilland, meant that Allied aircrews were no longer mere 'Fokker Fodder'. The pendulum swung back to the Germans towards the end of 1916 with the arrival of a new machine from the Albatros-Flugzeugwerke. This became completely dominant in the air in the coming months, especially during 'Bloody April' when the RFC and the French Air Service incurred heavy casualties during the Battle of Arras. Morale amongst airmen and ground crews hit a low ebb. All changed again when the Sopwith Camel – so called because of the hump in its fuselage – was introduced. By the war's end, it had accounted for 1,294 enemy aircraft.

This new type of warfare produced its own heroes and 'aces', an ace being dependent on the number of enemy planes a pilot had shot down, each kill recorded on his aircraft's fuselage. Amongst the most famous were the German Manfred von Richthofen (1892–1918) – known as the 'Red Baron' – the Frenchman Georges Guynemer (1894–1917) and the British pilot Albert Ball (1896–1917). All three men were killed in action.

The First World War made it evident that aircraft were now a vital part of any fighting force and their tactical use had the power to influence the result of battles being fought on the ground. The British recognised this in 1918, when the Royal Flying Corps and the Royal Naval Air Service were amalgamated to form the Royal Air Force, a separate branch of the armed forces.

Spies

The fevered atmosphere of pre-war Europe created a climate in which novels such as *The Riddle of the Sands* by writers such as Erskine Childers (1870–1922) and *A Secret Service* by William Le Queux (1864–1927) became hugely popular. They led to rumours of networks of German spies and a great deal of hysteria. The truth was that at that time there were no German spies operating in Britain. The outbreak of war changed that.

In 1909, the Secret Intelligence Bureau (SIB) was created in response to public concern about German spies operating in England. Major (later Colonel) Sir Vernon Kell (1873–1942), an expert in interrogation techniques, was appointed director of the newly created agency but in 1911, the various security services were reorganised, Kell's section becoming the Home Section. A new Foreign Section was introduced, known as the Secret Service Bureau and headed by Sir Mansfield Smith-Cumming (1859–1923). Smith-Cumming became known as 'C' over the next few years due to his habit of initialling papers he had read. It was a designation that was applied to all future directors. In charge of Naval Intelligence was master code-breaker Admiral Sir Reginald 'Blinker' Hall (1870–1943). With Sir Alfred Ewing (1855–1935), he established the Royal Navy's codebreaking operation, Room 40, which in 1917 would decode the Zimmermann telegram that contributed to America's entry into the war. His work made Naval Intelligence the pre-eminent British intelligence agency during the war. Meanwhile, Special Branch was headed by Sir Basil Thomson (1861–1939), a former prison governor and colonial administrator. The staunchly conservative Thomson was said by some to be more interested in the activities of subversives and agitators in Britain than he was in German spies.

Germany's spying operation in Britain was headed by Gustav Steinhauer (1870–1930) who had recruited his network before the war by writing to German businessmen living in the United Kingdom and inviting them to work for him. Other German spies entered Britain via the United States or other neutral countries using stolen or forged passports. They visited sensitive sites such as ports, shipyards and areas where military training was taking place, communicating with their operators by means of letters written in code with invisible ink. Between 1914 and 1917, only 31 German spies were arrested on British soil, 19 of whom were sentenced to death while the remainder were imprisoned. The first German spy to be executed in Britain demonstrates just how amateurish their attempts were. Carl Hans Lody (1877–1914) was executed in November 1914, having left a trail of clues behind him as he carried out his espionage. Most of the information he supplied to his masters was useless. One report claims that he informed his bosses that Russian troops had arrived in Scotland but he had in fact been speaking to some Scottish soldiers with strong accents and they had told him they were from 'Rosshire'.

Meanwhile, homing pigeons were killed in order to prevent them being used to carry messages to the enemy. There were also thousands of reports of 'night-signalling', spies signalling to Zeppelins or submarines to guide them to their targets. Hysterical accounts were given of enemy agents infecting cavalry horses with anthrax, starting fires at ports and even pretending to be circus performers or commercial travellers so that they could move around the country gathering intelligence. Eventually, in May 1915, the Asquith government decided to intern all 'enemy aliens' living in Britain for the duration of the war.

3

1915
Digging In

Do you remember the rats; and the stench
Of corpses rotting in front of the front-line trench-
And dawn coming, dirty-white, and chill with a hopeless rain?
Do you ever stop and ask, 'Is it all going to happen again?'
From 'Aftermath', by Siegfried Sassoon (1886–1967)

Total War

The failures of 1914 called into question the wisdom of persevering with the war. The general staffs on both sides had never foreseen such a conflict, so different to any that had gone before. No longer was it a struggle between armies; it was a fight to the death between entire societies, each leveraging their resources and their people. It was total war that brought privations and restrictions for those at home, hundreds and sometimes thousands of miles away from the fighting, as well as for those in direct contact with the enemy on the battlefield.

For the Germans, the nightmare scenario had come to pass. The very thing they had planned for years to avoid – a war on two fronts – was now a reality. Furthermore, their major ally, Austria-Hungary, was turning out to be shambolic. One German officer reflected the thoughts of many of his colleagues when he said having Austria-Hungary as an ally was like being shackled to a corpse. But Germany still had the advantage of being Europe's greatest military and industrial power and many of her factories had been converted to producing huge quantities of military hardware and ammunition. She also had the most professional army of all the warring nations, and had learned a great deal from her disappointments of the first year of the war. The army's heavy, mobile artillery and efficient armaments and equipment had allowed it to adapt to this new style of warfare and its communications network, a highly efficient railway system, gave her the capability to transfer her forces around the various theatres quickly.

Consequently, the task for the Allies appeared great. Russia, for instance, had inexhaustible reserves of manpower but was unable to equip her troops properly or get them to the front speedily enough. To try to alleviate some of the equipment problems, there was a rapid expansion of Russian industry, but it would be some time before Russian factories and foundries got up to speed. All the while, the inequalities and injustices of Russian society were becoming increasingly critical and this expansion of industry did little to relieve the situation.

The French and the British faced the German occupation of Belgium and northern France. In fact, the German trenches were a mere sixty miles from Paris itself and ten per cent of French soil was under occupation. It was now time for the French army to take over, the British regular army having effectively been wiped out. However, 855,000 French troops had already been killed, or were missing or wounded and they lacked the kind of mobile, heavy artillery being used to such good effect by the Germans. British Secretary of State for War, Herbert Kitchener (1850–1916), was in the process of creating what became known as the New Army or, occasionally, Kitchener's Army, a force of civilian volunteers that would be well trained and equipped but they would not be ready to take the field until 1916. The response to his appeal for volunteers was overwhelming and by the end of 1914, 1,186,337 men had signed up, a figure that rose to 2,257,521 by September 1915. More than two-thirds of the battalions created during the first two years of the war were Pals' Battalions, consisting of men who had enlisted together in local recruitment drives and who had been promised they would be able to serve alongside their colleagues and friends. Schools, sports clubs and trades formed battalions, the downside being, of course, that when heavy casualties were suffered by one of them, entire towns, villages, neighbourhoods and communities at home were badly affected.

Of course, such huge numbers of recruits presented the government with problems. The difficulty of providing shelter for so many men was alleviated by the construction of temporary accommodation at the main training camps but there was also a lack of equipment as well as suitable personnel to train the flood of recruits. Often men trained in their own clothing with regimental and unit badges sewn on, while some regiments raised money for uniforms through public subscription. Old uniforms, sometimes dating from the Boer War, were brought out of storage. Reserve-list officers were called up to train the recruits and British Indian Army officers home on leave were also brought in to help. Alumni of public schools and universities, many of whom had been members of Officer Training Corps, were often granted commissions without any prior training. Men in the ranks with leadership potential were promoted to meet the demand, especially later in the war when the casualty rate amongst junior infantry officers was extremely high. Equipment, too, was a problem, every piece available being used in the war. New artillery brigades trained with old rifles or wooden mock-ups. Such issues began to be dealt with, however, in the course of 1915.

An even worse crisis lay in the supply of munitions. The firms engaged to make weapons and ammunition were unused to the work, leading to orders being delayed and by the spring of 1915, munitions were being rationed, troops limited to just a few rounds per day. Sir John French leaked information about these shortages to *The Times* leading to a scandal that became known as the 'Shell Crisis'. Under the headline: 'Need for shells: British attacks checked: Limited supply the cause: A Lesson From France', was the comment: 'We had not sufficient high explosives to lower the enemy's parapets to the ground... The want of an unlimited supply of high explosives was a fatal bar to our success'. In May the 'Shell Crisis' brought down the Liberal government of Herbert Asquith, a coalition, with Asquith still as Prime Minister, taking power. In June, David Lloyd George (1863–1945) became Minister of Munitions, charged with the task of industrial mobilisation. There was a radical change of thinking, the government finally conceding that if the Allies were to have any chance of victory, the entire British economy would have to be geared for war. As Lloyd George said in a speech that summer:

'It is a war of munitions. We are fighting against the best organised community in the world, the best organised either for peace or war, and we have been employing too much the haphazard, leisurely, go-as-you-please methods, which, believe me, would not have enabled us to maintain our place as a nation even in peace very much longer... We must increase the mobility of labour, and... we must have greater subordination in labour to the direction and control of the state.'

The Home Front

The change in Britain at this time was extraordinary. The servant class began to diminish, men enlisting in the armed forces and women going out to work, sometimes in munitions factories. Indeed, women were taking over many traditional male roles – there were women bus drivers and conductors and they worked on the railways as porters and guards while government offices were filled with middle-class women. Behaviour changed, too. The prospect of men going away to die encouraged love affairs and the death-knell for the Victorian notion of female chastity. Even the way women dressed underwent something of a revolution, hemlines rising and the corset being consigned to history.

Britain had always been isolated from the horrors of European war by the English Channel and the North Sea. Now for the first time, modern technology had removed that protection. On 19 January 1915, two Zeppelin airships attacked the eastern coastal towns of Great Yarmouth and King's Lynn, killing four civilians but causing little significant damage. The first Zeppelin attack on London killed seven people on 31 May. Later in the year there were more costly attacks, such as on the night of 13–14 October when five Zeppelins were responsible for the deaths of 71 people. The Zeppelin, however, was vulnerable to poor weather conditions and its size made it an ideal target for British fighter pilots and anti-aircraft guns. From spring 1917, the Germans would turn to planes such as the Gotha that were able to fly long distances. On 13 June 1917, 20 Gothas killed 162 civilians in London, the highest death toll from a single air raid during the war. Such incidents increased anti-German feeling amongst British civilians.

In July 1915, Welsh coal miners went on strike, demanding an increase in their wages rather than the 'war bonus' that was being paid by the government, a payment that the miners suspected would be withdrawn as soon as the conflict ended. Coal was, of course, in great demand, and the owners of the mines were making huge profits, none of which, the miners complained, was being passed on to them. The strike caused problems for all, since coal was the primary source of fuel for both houses and industry, but it was of particular concern for the Royal Navy which required huge quantities of coal to keep its ships at sea. After less than a week of industrial action, the government was forced to intervene, sending Munitions Minister, and Welshman, Lloyd George to negotiate with the strike leaders. The strike ended on 20 July when the government conceded to the strikers' demands and the miners returned to work.

The Eastern Front; German Offensives and Austrian Failures

The Eastern Front differed greatly from the Western. To begin with, in the west at the start of 1915, 100 German divisions lined up against 110 from the Allies. In the east – defending a line more than double the length of the Western Front – the Central Powers had only 80 divisions to 83 Russian. The same applied to weaponry; there was a great deal more firepower in the west and for that reason trench warfare did not develop to the same extent in the east. There were insufficient numbers of men to make a continuous trench system work. Roads and railways, too, presented a different set of problems. The Russians had great difficulty in getting troops quickly to the front. They did not possess any lateral railway lines that could transport troops from north to south or vice-versa. Behind their own lines, the Germans were well served with railways, but, of course, once they started to advance into enemy territory, that advantage was lost. Frustratingly for them, their line gauge was different to that of Russia. It was usual, therefore, for the Germans with their superior weaponry and more professional army, to make significant advances into Russian territory, to hesitate when they lost touch with their supply lines and then to be faced with Russian reserves that had finally been brought forward by the ponderous Russian war machine. Thus, the conflict in the east became as much of a stalemate as it was in the west.

Falkenhayn wanted to make gains in the west, correctly surmising that victory could only come if Germany gained superiority in that theatre. Hindenburg and Ludendorff were buoyant, however, after their successes and wanted to press home their advantage in the east. Meanwhile, it was plainly obvious that without reinforcements, the Austro-Hungarians would be unable to hold their line in the Carpathians. Reluctantly, the German commander decided to remain defensive in the west and mount the offensive against the Russians that Hindenburg and Ludendorff had chosen – in Masuria. Meanwhile, Conrad, the Austro-Hungarian commander, wanted German reinforcements to bolster his own beleaguered force and push out of the Carpathians towards the fortress of Przemysl where 120,000 of his men were besieged. On 23 January 1915, the campaign in the Carpathians was launched. Conrad's troops advanced but they were held up as rugged terrain and deep snow prevented them from being supplied. With soldiers starving and freezing to death and attacks by wolves taking the lives of some, the advance halted. A further three initiatives, two Russian and another Austro-Hungarian also failed to achieve their objectives and Przemysl remained under siege. Austro-Hungarian casualties now totalled 400,000 and 120,000, including nine generals, were captured when Przemysl eventually capitulated on 23 March. The future effectiveness of the army was also destroyed by the loss of a huge number of officers and NCOs.

Meanwhile, in the north the Germans went on the offensive, driving the Russian army back some 70 miles. Only resolute resistance on the right by the Russian Twelfth Army prevented them being encircled. It was another tremendous success for Hindenburg and Ludendorff, although their advance from one side of the Masurian Lakes to the other had again extended their supply lines. They inflicted 200,000 casualties on the Russians, a great deal more than their own tally.

In the south of the Eastern Front, the Austro-Hungarian armies had now suffered a staggering 2 million casualties and it was known that Italy was negotiating to join the ranks of the Entente against the Central Powers, a decision that could prove catastrophic for the Hapsburgs. Conrad even hinted that a negotiated peace might be the only solution for them. Instead, Falkenhayn dispatched eight divisions to the east to create a new Eleventh Army commanded by General August von Mackensen (1849–1945) that arrived clandestinely between the towns of Gorlice and Tarnow. The Central Powers had eighteen divisions, ten German in the centre and eight Austro-Hungarian on the flanks. Facing them were a mere five and a half Russian divisions of dubious fighting quality. The plan was to destroy the Russians here before wheeling north to expel the Russian troops in the Polish salient towards Hindenburg's forces in East Prussia. On 2 May the bombardment began, lasting for four hours and destroying the meagre Russian defences of shallow ditches and small stretches of barbed wire. By evening a gap five miles wide had been blasted in the Russian lines and within a couple of weeks the Germans had advanced 100 miles. Przemysl was re-captured on 3 June and on

20 June a full Russian retreat from Galicia was ordered. Mackensen pursued the Russians across the River Dnieper while Hindenburg launched an attack in the north. Warsaw fell on 4–5 August.

Having advanced an astonishing 300 miles, however, the Germans found themselves with the same old problem. Their railheads were still anywhere between 50 and 100 miles behind the front and supplies had to be transported on horseback or on trucks the remainder of the distance. As the German troops became exhausted and even the supply of water became tenuous, the Russians, closer to their supplies, were able to get fresh troops to the front. The advance was halted but the statistics were staggering. The Russians had lost almost a million, killed or wounded, 850,000 had been taken prisoner and by September, 3,000 Russian guns had been captured. It is unknown how many troops the Germans lost, but it was certainly a lot fewer than the Russians. The Russian threat was now, effectively, over and Falkenhayn was free to concentrate his efforts on the Western Front.

New Combatants

It had always been fairly inevitable, given the outcome of the Second Balkan War, that Bulgaria, faced with Allied support for its rival Serbia, would take the side of the Central Powers. In 1916, Romania joined the Entente Powers, as did Greece a year later. Of more significance was the entry of Turkey into the war. The Ottoman Empire was very much in decline but her strategic importance could not be overestimated. At the Dardanelles, she could block entry into the Black Sea and also posed a threat to Egypt and the Suez Canal. This had, of course, long been understood by Britain and Germany and both had made efforts prior to the war to bring Turkey into their sphere of influence. The Germans had built the Berlin to Baghdad railway and had provided officers to help train and modernise the Turkish army. Turkey had been eager to own dreadnought-type ships and the British had agreed to build two for them. As they were nearing completion, however, at the start of the war, Winston Churchill, as First Lord of the Admiralty, ordered them to be seized. The Turks were furious with the British, especially as the money to pay for them had been raised by public subscription. The Germans sensed an opportunity. In August 1914, two German battlecruisers, SMS *Goeben* and SMS *Breslau*, slipped past the Royal Navy's Mediterranean Fleet and took refuge at Constantinople, then capital of the Turkish Empire, at that point still neutral. The Germans offered the ships to the Turks as compensation for the vessels that Churchill had seized, hoping this gesture would force Turkey out of her neutral position and onto their side. Churchill, from that point onwards considered the Turks to be enemies, ordering the ships to be sunk, whether they were sailing under a Turkish flag or a German one. The Turks responded by closing the Dardanelles, preventing armaments from reaching Russia's Black Sea ports and within a week, Britain, France and Russia had all declared war on Turkey. The Turks invaded the Russian province of the Caucasus with the oilfields at Baku their primary objective, but their troops, unprepared for the difficult winter conditions, were heavily defeated.

In early 1915, Russian forces crossed the border into the largely Christian north-western Turkish province of Armenia. The Armenians, under Ottoman control since the fifteenth and sixteenth centuries, had long demanded self-determination. The Turks, meanwhile, sought an even greater Turkish Empire and were unlikely to want to lose a part of it. When the Turkish army was defeated by the Russians at the Battle of Sarikamish that was fought from December 1914 until January 1915, the Turkish leader, Enver Pasha (1881–1922) publicly blamed the defeat on the collaboration with the Russians of Armenians in the region. Turkish soldiers began slaughtering Armenians and plundering their villages. In Constantinople, on 24 April 1915, 250 Armenian intellectuals and community leaders were arrested. Many were subsequently thrown from ships in the Bosphorus and drowned. Across Turkey, Armenian men, women and children of all ages were tortured, raped, starved and butchered or were deported to Syria and Mosul. They were subjected to forced labour and death marches in the Syrian Desert and women were often given the option of choosing Islam or death. This, one of the first modern genocides, resulted in a death toll of between 1 and 1.5 million Armenians.

The Italian people were divided over which side they should join. Italy was, as always, suspicious of the French and was, of course, a member of the Triple Alliance. On 26 April, however, Italy secretly signed the Treaty of London, agreeing to leave the Triple Alliance, join the Entente and declare war on Germany and Austria-Hungary. In fact, the Italians declared war on Austria-Hungary on 23 May, but it was not until 1916 that war was declared on Germany. It is worth pointing out that there was never any real chance that Italy would fight alongside the Central Powers. Her vulnerability to sea blockades and her dependence on Britain for supplies of coal guaranteed this. Furthermore, there were territorial gains to be made at the expense of Austria-Hungary – Tyrol, Trieste, Istria and a section of the Dalmatian coast. Also included in the secret agreement was the fact that Albania would become an independent Muslim state but that she would be a protectorate of the Italians who would oversee her foreign policy.

There were also benefits for the Allies in having Italy join them. They would gain crucial Mediterranean bases while the new front would draw Austro-Hungarian forces away from the Eastern Front. The Italian army, however, would prove totally unprepared for war. It lacked modern artillery and machine guns and its officers were of poor quality. To add to its problems, the region in which it would be fighting – its 400-mile border with Austria-Hungary – was almost entirely mountainous, the Austrians having taken up defensive positions not on the frontier, but on high ground beyond it. The Italians wasted no time, however, in going on the attack, Italian Chief of Staff General Luigi Cadorna (1850–1928) ordering his troops onto the offensive on the plateau made by the River Isonzo, the area with most potential for an attack. All told, there were twelve battles at Isonzo between 1915 and 1917. By the end of the third, which ended on 3 November, the Italians had suffered 125,000 casualties, the Austrians 100,000. It had all proved futile, however, because the line had barely changed.

The Fall of Serbia

The Germans were beginning to realise that they were probably going to have to get their hands dirty in the east. Despite the Italians' lack of progress, the Austro-Hungarians were not faring well and, as we will see, Turkey was also coming under threat from the Allies. Falkenhayn decided that Serbia was the weak point where some advantage could be gained and some good news could be sent back home to a public hungry for it. He decided that Germany would play the principal role in this offensive and it did not take much to persuade Bulgaria into the conflict on the side of the Central Powers – namely the restoration of the territory it had lost to the Serbians in the Second Balkan War of 1913.

The Serbs had seen off Austrian offensives in 1914 and by the end of the year were ready to go on the offensive and send the invaders back across the border. The German entry into this theatre soon put a halt to that notion. Led by General Mackensen, the Central Powers caught the Serbs in a pincer movement launched on 7 October – the Germans and Austro-Hungarians in the north and the Bulgarians in the south. The Serbs put up stubborn resistance, holding back Conrad's force and allowing the Bulgarians to make only slow progress. It was just a matter of time, though, and soon the Serbian army was engaged in an epic retreat that took them over the mountains of Albania to the Adriatic coast from where Entente ships carried 150,000 of them to the Greek island of Corfu.

The British and French had quickly assembled a force that landed at Salonika in Greece on 5 September. When they found themselves unable to break out past the Bulgarians, they dug in, becoming known as the 'Gardeners of Salonika'. It is said that the British wanted to withdraw, but French commander General Joffre refused to order his men to come home. The cynical view has it that he was reluctant to allow the commander of the expedition, General Maurice Sarrail (1856–1929), to return to France because he feared Sarrail was a threat to his position. Falkenhayn sarcastically described the Allied emplacement at Salonika as the biggest internment camp in the world.

The Disaster of Gallipoli

The first major operation by the British against Turkey was aimed at re-opening trade access to Russia through the Black Sea. It was also hoped that it would remove Turkey as a force in the war. First

Lord of the Admiralty Winston Churchill was of the belief that the navy could be used to influence the war on land and had been searching for an opportunity to prove this. His admirals, on the other hand, were fearful that such an action would put the Grand Fleet at risk of destruction by enemy mines, submarines and torpedo-boats. The Russians, struggling against the Turks in the Caucasus, had requested help from Kitchener and Churchill saw his opportunity, devising a plan to force a way through the Dardanelles Straits using old and expendable battleships. These ships would make their way to Constantinople, threaten the city and persuade the Turks to withdraw from the war. He estimated that such an action would influence those Balkan states that remained neutral to align themselves with the powers of the Entente, providing a new threat to Austria-Hungary and Germany from the south-east. The scheme was given the go-ahead and on 19 February 1915, ships of the Royal Navy opened fire on the outer forts of the Dardanelles. Although a number of guns were destroyed, when it came to the large guns in the forts at the Narrows, defended by minefields and mobile howitzers, the fleet was unable to make an impact. On 18 March, as an attack intended to clear the mines and destroy the forts was launched, HMS *Inflexible* was seriously damaged and HMS *Irresistible* was sunk, and the French battleships *Suffren* and *Gaulois* were badly damaged. There was an opportunity to call off the action at this point, but instead Kitchener ordered that a military force be dispatched to the Dardanelles to occupy the Gallipoli Peninsula with the ultimate aim of rendering the forts ineffective and allowing the ships to continue to Constantinople to complete their mission. Luckily, there was a force of around 70,000 troops in the vicinity of the Dardanelles – a naval division; a regular Army division, Australian and New Zealand troops who would famously become known as

'Anzacs'; and a division of French soldiers. General Sir Ian Hamilton (1853–1947), put in command of this force, quickly made plans for a landing to take place on 25 April. The 29th Division landed at Cape Helles, located at the tip of the peninsula, with the job of advancing on the Kilid Bahr Plateau and attacking the forts at the Narrows. To the north, the Anzacs were to land and traverse the peninsula, preventing Turkish reinforcements from attacking the 29th. The French would stage a landing on the Asiatic shore, close to Kum Kale.

It went wrong from the outset, the 29th Division battling underwater obstructions as they attempted to make a landing, forcing the troops to disembark in the sea. All the while they were under constant fire from Turkish emplacements that had been left unscathed by bombardment from the ships. They succeeded in taking the beach by nightfall, but were unable to effect any further advance for the moment. There were problems for the Anzacs as well. They had erroneously been landed a mile further north than intended and their route off the beach was sharply inclined and peppered with deep ravines. Many, including large numbers of junior officers, were cut down by Turkish guns. Maps that had been provided proved inaccurate and there was a general state of confusion, giving the Turks time to organise themselves. Reinforcements in the next few days resulted in small advances and the establishment of a defensive perimeter that helped to drive back, at huge cost, a major Turkish attack on 19 May, but there was little hope of advancing. The British and French forces at Cape Helles failed countless times between late April and early June to break through the Turkish defences and trench warfare ensued with trenches often less than 100 metres apart. The fighting was frequently hand-to-hand and grim in the extreme. Trenches were often blocked with corpses, the smell of decaying flesh an ever-present reminder of the desperate situation. Swarms of flies made life difficult and deadly malaria, dysentery and other stomach disorders took just as many casualties as bullets and bombs. The heat of summer was overwhelming and there was never enough water. Even if the wounded were evacuated and made it onto ships, medical staff were inadequately trained and the shortage of fit men led to many being sent back to the trenches before they were well enough.

In August in the north of the peninsula, the Anzacs assaulted Turkish troops who were dug in on a ridge while a new force was landed on their left to capture the level ground around Suvla Bay with the intention of using this spot as a supply base. The Anzacs failed to reach the ridge before darkness fell, allowing the Turks to bring up reinforcements and once again the Allies failed to break through. Eventually, doubts were raised about General Hamilton's abilities, leading to his replacement by General Sir Charles Monro (1860–1929) who immediately concluded that the Gallipoli Campaign should be brought to an end. Churchill was particularly dismayed by this decision. 'He came, he saw, he capitulated', he commented. On 19–20 December troops evacuated Anzac Cove, Cape Helles being cleared of Allied troops the following month.

The Gallipoli Campaign was a costly failure. The Allies suffered 250,000 casualties, the Turks double that number. Nonetheless, it had consequences that reached far beyond the First World War. For Turks, whose troops had proved a good deal more courageous and effective than the Allies had given them credit for, the victory represents a defining moment in their history, forming the basis for the Turkish War of Independence that followed the end of the war and the 1923 founding of the Republic of Turkey, led by Mustafa Kemal Atatürk (1881–1938), a commander at Gallipoli. It was also important to Australia and New Zealand, often believed to have marked the birth of national consciousness for those two young nations. The date of the landing of the Anzacs is known as 'Anzac Day' and is commemorated each year in those countries.

Meanwhile, when a coalition government was formed in May 1915, Churchill lost his position at the Admiralty primarily because of his championing of the campaign in Gallipoli. After serving as Chancellor of the Duchy of Lancaster for a few months, he resigned from the government and rejoined the British army as a lieutenant colonel. He served on the Western Front for several months before returning to the House of Commons.

The Western Front

In 1915, almost all of Belgium and a substantial part of France were under German occupation. German troops were dangerously close to the coast and the Channel ports that were of such importance to the British war effort. There was no question, therefore, of the Allies releasing troops to fight in another theatre. They could not afford to give the Germans any excuse to launch a major assault in the west. For the French commander-in-chief, General Joffre, the way forward had to be to drive the Germans back to their own borders with mass assaults through Belgium; in other words, more of the same tactics that had failed so signally in 1914. Meanwhile, two powerful figures in the British government – Winston Churchill and David Lloyd George – argued against such a strategy, citing the cost in numbers of casualties as a major reason. Lloyd George championed, instead, an attack on one of the Central Powers' allies, in the Balkans or the Middle East, describing it as an opportunity to 'knock the props out from under Germany'. But there was never any chance of this happening.

The British army at the time had neither the trained soldiers

71

nor the weaponry to mount an independent assault. Therefore, it could only be effective in conjunction with the French. This gave Joffre a large say in how the war was prosecuted. Unfortunately, he does not seem to have had any answer to the problem of breaking through the securely entrenched German lines, despite the valiant efforts of his troops to do so. On 10 March, there was a plan for British and French troops to mount an assault on Aubers Ridge, but the French withdrew their force, leaving the British to mount their first independent action on the Western Front. After bombarding the enemy lines, they advanced as far as the village of Neuve Chapelle. However, they were unable to exploit their success, especially in view of a shortage of artillery shells. The Germans responded by strengthening their defences in the area but the French were at least reassured that the British could be effective in offensive operations.

The Germans remained on the defensive in the west in 1915 but they had come up with an offensive innovation that they hoped would give them an advantage – poison gas. It had already been tried against the Russians and had failed but on 22 April, during the Second Battle of Ypres, they tried it again, directing it towards French soldiers and then Canadians. Its delivery was very basic. It arrived at the front line in cylinders and was released when the wind began to blow in the right direction. When combined with water, chlorine gas makes hypochlorous acid that destroys tissue, such as lungs and eyes. It is denser than air and rapidly filled the trenches. Panicked troops fled into the open where they were mown down by enemy fire. There were approximately 6,000 casualties amongst French troops from the gas, many dying in minutes from asphyxiation and damage to the lungs, while many more were blinded. From May to June there were 350 British deaths from gas poisoning. Soon, however, troops were improvising protective measures, such as masks, that became increasingly sophisticated as the war continued. Of course, the use of gas was a tremendous opportunity for the Allies' PR machine, to emphasise the barbarity of the enemy. Before long, such considerations were forgotten as the Allies themselves began to use poison gas.

Ready to mount a large operation by April, Joffre chose to stage it in Artois, in the sector of the front that stretched from Vimy Ridge to Arras. Here, the Germans were thinly spread, many having been sent east to support the Hapsburg efforts. The objective was to seize the ridge, open the plain of Douai to cavalry and take control of the rail system while the British attacked in the north. It was to be a very concentrated attack with more than 1,000 guns employed, 300 of which were heavy artillery, and 13 divisions would be brought to bear on just 20 miles of front. There were just four German divisions opposing them.

The guns bombarded the German lines from 6 to 9 May, aiming at trenches and the German batteries located on the other side of the ridge. There was immediate success against German troops taken by surprise despite the seven-day bombardment, but it was brief. The guns had failed to knock out the German artillery and heavy casualties were suffered by a division of French-Moroccan soldiers who initially reached the top of Vimy Ridge but were driven back. That was the extent of the success of the initiative and no progress was made at any other part of the offensive. Repeated attacks throughout the remainder of that month also failed. In the middle of June, a major advance was planned using fresh troops but it was halted by a German barrage. The French-Moroccans again took the ridge and were again forced to retreat when it was learned that the reserves who should have been brought in to support them were too far back. The spring 1915 offensive had cost the disappointed Joffre 100,000 casualties while the Germans lost 60,000.

Despite the failure, Joffre remained confident. Perhaps, after all, if those reserves had been closer to the front along with heavy guns, victory might have been his. He was also encouraged by the continuing shortage of manpower from which the Germans were suffering. Others were less ebullient and a June meeting of Allied munitions experts concluded that it would be impossible to manufacture enough munitions and guns to enable an autumn offensive. Neither did Joffre have the support of the British commander-in-chief Sir John French who was reluctant to have another failure such as had been experienced at Aubers Ridge. However, given the disasters on the Eastern Front, there was little left to do but let Joffre persevere with his approach. British Minister of War, Lord Kitchener, was pragmatic. 'Unfortunately, we have to make war as we must,' he said in August 1915, 'and not as we should like.'

The autumn campaign would focus on Champagne and Artois, the objective being to seize the German communications system, located some fifty miles behind the front line. In Champagne, Joffre assembled eighteen divisions along a twenty-mile front, supported by 700 heavy guns, 25 per cent of all the French heavy weapons on the Western Front. Meanwhile, in Artois, eleven French and five British divisions would be supported by 420 heavy guns. Reserves and cavalry massed behind the troops. In Champagne, the Allied troops faced only seven divisions and in Artois the Germans could muster only six. But they had not been standing still since the spring and they boasted a much more robust trench network, a second line of trenches having been dug a couple of miles behind the front, often located on a site sloping away from the front, making it difficult for artillery to be effective against them. Nonetheless, they still suffered from a serious lack of manpower. The French heavy artillery initially made light work of the German defences, allowing troops to overrun the German first line. They attacked the second line on a five-mile front but without the help of artillery, now too far behind them, they encountered difficulties. When three divisions of German troops arrived, the French attack ground to a halt, much to the relief of a panicked Falkenhayn.

In Artois, there was inadequate softening of the German defences by artillery and soldiers were hampered by intact barbed wire and machine gun posts. The British fared slightly better, helped by Sir John French's decision to unleash poison gas, although it did stray into the path of many of his own troops. Nonetheless, the British succeeded in crossing no man's land under cover of the gas and the smoke of battle, and with German troops being withdrawn to provide support against the French, they captured the German first line along a four-mile front and took the village of Loos. The following day, however, two British divisions were decimated after a foolhardy order by French for them to attack a German line that knew they were coming. They suffered 8,000 casualties and shortly after French was persuaded to resign. He was replaced by General Sir Douglas Haig (1861–1928) who was at the time commander of the First Army.

Joffre's September offensive had cost around 200,000 Allied casualties, against German losses of 85,000. The sum total of the ground gained as a result of the Allies' constant attacks was about 2000 yards along a 12- to 14-mile front. The Germans simply made their second line the front line and dug another line of trenches a few miles behind them to act as a new second line.

The War at Sea and the Sinking of the *Lusitania*

For centuries people had been dreaming of a craft that was capable of independent operation under water. The advantages, especially in time of war, were obvious – the ability to take the enemy unawares, to spy unseen and to submerge quickly and vanish if spotted by the enemy. Midway through the nineteenth century, the first air-independent and combustion-powered submarines were being designed. Their suitability for warfare was confirmed with the development of the earliest practical self-propelled torpedoes, the first designed by British engineer Robert Whitehead (1823–1905) in 1866. The first submarines to go into operational service were steam-powered British K-class vessels that were designed in 1913. Unfortunately, they were involved in so many accidents that they were nicknamed 'Kalamity class'. Germany's diesel-powered U-boats were better designed and far more reliable. Both the K-boat and the U-boat carried torpedoes, but their main offensive weapons were their deck guns that meant they had to rise to the surface to engage an enemy ship. In time, K-class vessels were superseded by the more modern E-class submarines, powered by diesel turbines on the surface and an electric motor when submerged.

At the outbreak of hostilities, the Germans had only 30 U-boats in service. The first action in which one engaged ended badly for it, HMS *Birmingham* sinking U-15 although this was avenged by the sinking of HMS *Pathfinder* a month later by U-21. Early in the war, U-boats would surface to fire on British merchant vessels but on such occasions, they would allow the crews of the targeted ships to disembark into lifeboats and escape before opening fire on and sinking their ships. This soon changed, however, following the launch by German naval command of a policy of unrestricted submarine warfare, declaring the waters around Britain to be a 'war zone'. Ships that were found in these waters were now liable to be fired on and sunk without prior warning. In 1915, German U-boats sank almost 1.4 million tons of Allied shipping.

The British ocean liner the RMS *Lusitania* had been launched by the Cunard line in 1907. She had briefly been the biggest ship in the world and was the fastest on the transatlantic service, fitted with turbine engines capable of a speed of 25 knots. Warning had been given by the German embassy in New York that the ship was likely to be attacked under Germany's new unrestricted submarine warfare policy. The liner steamed out of New York on 1 May 1915 and six days later was torpedoed by the German U-boat U-20 off the coast of southern Ireland, inside the 'war zone'. There was a second explosion inside the ship and within 18 minutes she had sunk, taking with her 1,098 passengers and crew, 128 of whom were Americans.

The sinking created an understandable outcry and a wave of protest in the United States. Britain thought that the USA should declare war on Germany as a result of the sinking, but President Woodrow Wilson (1856–1924) reacted cautiously. In correspondence with the United States government, however, the German Foreign Minister Gottlieb von Jagow argued that the *Lusitania* was a legitimate military target because she was listed as an armed merchant cruiser, she flew neutral flags and had been issued with orders to ram any German submarines she encountered. He added that on previous voyages, *Lusitania* was known to have carried Allied troops and munitions. The *Lusitania* was, in fact, officially listed as carrying amongst her cargo rifle and machine-gun ammunition, shrapnel artillery shells without powder charges and artillery fuses. Wilson insisted on an apology from the German government and compensation for the victims' families, but still, to the dismay of the British government, he refused to take America into the war. Eventually, on 9 September 1915, the Germans announced that attacks would be permitted only on vessels that were definitely British. Neutral ships would be treated under Prize Law rules and would therefore, be captured, not sunk. Attacks on passenger liners were prohibited. The British attempted to keep passions enflamed in America, publishing an erroneous story that German schoolchildren were given a holiday in celebration of the sinking. The incident undoubtedly made the American people more supportive of the Allied cause and was a contributory factor in the decisive entry of the United States into the war in 1917.

1915: In Conclusion

1915 had been a disappointing year for the Allies. Admittedly, the entry of the Italians into the war on their side had provided hope but the Italians had not yet produced much to concern the Central Powers. In the east, the Russians had suffered humiliating defeats and had lost a lot of territory. In the Balkans, Bulgaria had sided with the Central Powers and Serbia had been defeated. The Allies' efforts on this front had done little but remove forces from where they were really needed. Critically, on the Western Front, the Germans had held their ground despite having to withdraw troops to fight in the east. They had also succeeded in inflicting heavy casualties on the British and the French who had gained almost nothing from the year.

Nonetheless, the task facing Germany as the year ended looked increasingly daunting. Not only were the French mobilising both men and machinery but Britain was also beginning to harness the not inconsiderable power of her industry and the support of her empire. Meanwhile, the Royal Navy still reigned supreme at sea, despite the success of German U-boats, enabling the British to exploit trading opportunities with neutral countries, especially the United States, and maintain a blockade on an increasingly hungry German people.

4

1916
A New Kind of Hell

'What passing-bells for these who die as cattle?
Only the monstrous anger of the guns.'
From 'Anthem for Doomed Youth', by Wilfred Owen

The War at Sea: the Battle of Jutland

The Battle of Jutland was the only major naval battle of the war. Both navies had managed to avoid confrontation, on the whole, since the start of the conflict, but on 31 May 1916, they finally faced each other off the coast of Jutland in the North Sea in one of history's largest naval battles. Known to the Germans as the Battle of Skagerrak, its combatants were a German fleet under the command of Vice-Admiral Reinhard Scheer (1863–1928) and a British fleet commanded by Admiral Jellicoe.

Recognising that their fleet was not in a position to engage the entire British fleet, the German High Seas Fleet's commanders devised a plan to lure Vice-Admiral Sir David Beatty's (1871–1936) battlecruiser squadron out of Rosyth, in the belief that it was in pursuit of a relatively small German force. Instead, it would steam into the path of the main German fleet stationed fifty miles off the Scottish coast. Submarines were additionally positioned across the routes that the British ships were likely to sail. The Germans were unaware, however, that the British had access to their secret codes and had intercepted signals discussing the operation. On 30 May, therefore, Jellicoe sailed the Grand Fleet to rendezvous with Beatty, actually steaming over the unprepared German submarines, now reaching the limit of the time they could remain at sea. On the afternoon of 31 May, Beatty engaged with Vice-Admiral Franz Hipper's (1863–1932) five ships earlier than the Germans expected. Beatty was successfully drawn towards the main German fleet and lost two battlecruisers – HMS *Indefatigable* and HMS *Queen Mary* – from his force of six battlecruisers and four battleships. He then turned his ships back towards the main British force, the German fleet in hot pursuit. As the Germans came face to face with the main British fleet at around 18.30, Jellicoe ordered his ships, approaching in six lines, to turn to port. They formed a line and fired relentless broadsides at the German vessels. Horrified, and fearful that he might lose his entire force, Scheer ordered his ships to retire. The two sides – numbering 250 ships – engaged each other again later that evening but, although Jellicoe had positioned some of his ships to cut off the German retreat, they managed to break through the British line in the dark and make their way back to port.

Both sides claimed victory, but the British had lost more ships, fourteen to Germany's eleven and lost more than twice as many sailors – 6,094 killed against 2,551 Germans. The British press was critical of Jellicoe's failure to gain a decisive victory but it should also be pointed out that the German plan had been made to fail. Nonetheless, debate continues today over the performances of Jellicoe and Beatty that day. One thing that the battle confirmed was that Germany's policy of avoiding direct contact with the Royal Navy was wise. British command of the sea was never again challenged, and the German High Seas Fleet remained penned up in its ports for the remainder of the war. As one newspaper commented, 'The German fleet has assaulted its jailer, but is still in jail'.

The Western Front: Planning for 1916

The last months of 1915 had been relatively quiet on the Western Front as both sides decided their strategies for the following year. In December 1915, the Allies met at Chantilly to discuss strategy for the following year. Agreement was reached for a series of combined offensives against the Central Powers by the French, British, Italian and Russian armies. It was decided with commendable unanimity, that the offensives would take place simultaneously, thus preventing the Germans from moving their armies around Europe to wherever the greatest danger lay. The action on the Western Front, it was concluded, would take place at the River Somme during the summer of 1916. The delay until then was to allow Britain sufficient time to train and equip its 'Kitchener armies' of volunteers. It would also allow the Russians to recover from the disasters of 1915 and to gear their industry up for the production of armaments and equipment. Britain and France would attack the Germans on the Western Front simultaneously with a Russian offensive against the Germans on their northern front. Meanwhile, other Russian forces would attack the Austro-Hungarians on their south-western front and the Italians would hit them at the River Isonzo, this dual assault on the Hapsburg armies hopefully proving decisive.

Germany remained engaged in a war on two fronts, but the previous year had proved that this was a less perilous situation than had been feared. Austria-Hungary remained unreliable as an ally, but German armies in the east had dealt the Russians several hard blows and it was apparent that it would be some time before they could sufficiently recover and once again pose a serious threat. This allowed Falkenhayn to concentrate all his efforts on the Western Front. The question was as ever, of course, how to break the stalemate created by the elaborate trench systems and huge quantities of defensive artillery in that theatre. Joffre had not succeeded in 1915 with repeated efforts. Why would it be any different for the Germans if they went on the offensive in 1916?

All the authorities in the conflict seem to have come to the same conclusion at this time, however. They argued that the reason for Joffre's failures was a lack of sufficient high explosive shells. Falkenhayn believed that Germany had rectified this failing with increased industrial mobilisation. He planned therefore to stockpile a huge quantity of shells that he would unleash on the French lines, wiping them out. Although he believed the British to be the major obstacle to a German victory, he thought the best strategy was to first defeat the French. He estimated that by January 1916, the Allies would have 139 divisions in France and Belgium, against just 117 on the German side. But he was optimistic because he believed the French to be close to the 'limits of endurance', as he put it. He was certain they could be defeated in the coming year and, in that situation, Britain would have no other option than to sue for peace. He was no longer intent on the implausible mass breakthrough that had been the objective of both sides during the previous two years, planning instead to attack the French at a place that had such great significance to them that they would defend it to the last man. It would be a war of attrition in which capturing enemy lines, making advances or seizing territory would be rendered secondary to the principal aim of destroying the French army. As he explained in a memorandum to the Kaiser:

'There are objectives within our reach... for which the French General Staff would be forced to throw in every man they have. If they do so, the forces of France will be bled to death, since there can be no question of voluntary withdrawal... the objectives of which I speak are Belfort and Verdun... the preference must be given to Verdun.'

The Battle of Verdun

In a pre-Roman Gallic dialect, the word 'Verdun' means 'powerful fortress' and, indeed, the region had been fortified since Roman times. The Meuse River flowed through this strategically vital city that boasted 60 individual forts and outposts and miles of underground tunnels. Fort Douaumont, the largest of the forts was spread over nearly eight acres and was defended by a garrison of between 500 and 800 soldiers. For France it had great symbolic value. It was where Charlemagne had divided his empire up between his sons, creating the basis for the future states of France and Germany. Twice it had valiantly withstood German sieges – in 1792 and during the humiliating defeat of 1870 – before eventually capitulating. Painted on the door of Fort Douaumont's main entrance was the legend: 'Better to be buried under the ruins of the fort than to surrender it'. The loss of Verdun would, therefore, be a major blow to French morale, ensuring it would be defended no matter the cost. Its loss, Falkenhayn believed, would bring such a crisis that the French government would collapse. He would lay siege to the city for as long as it took and would kill as many French soldiers as he could.

Verdun had already distinguished itself during this war. It had been held during the Battle of the Marne, being the Allies' easternmost position. Maurice Sarrail's stout defence left it at the apex of a salient jutting deeply into German-held territory. Both sides fought vigorously for an advantage in the first half of 1915 but it remained unsullied. The fortifications, however, were not as strong as they appeared, French generals having lost faith in such defences following the destruction by the Germans of Belgium's forts. They were in a state of some disrepair, therefore, with inadequate trench systems between them. To make matters worse, Joffre had wrongly calculated that Verdun would remain quiet for a while and had removed its heavy guns. Meanwhile, he concentrated on his own plans for a 1916 offensive along the Somme, guessing wrongly that the Germans would do nothing for the first half of the year.

The German attack was launched on the morning of 21 February 1916 with a nine-hour bombardment of the French lines by the heaviest artillery concentration of the war thus far, some 1,600 artillery pieces. The first attempt to break through was driven back by resolute French resistance and it took until 25 February for Fort Douaumont to fall. The shaken French appointed a new commander of the armies at Verdun. Marshal Philippe Pétain (1856–1951), scion of a wealthy family from the Pas-de-Calais, was tasked with restoring the morale of his soldiers and driving the German offensive back. Pétain was adept at defensive warfare and amassed a huge array of French artillery on the left bank of the Meuse that rained shells on the Germans. One problem he encountered was that there was only one way into Verdun, a road dubbed 'La Voie Sacrée' ('The Sacred Way'), but even so, although it was constantly shelled, more than 25,000 tons of supplies and 190,000 men were carried along it in one week. These reinforcements were thrown into 'the furnace' as the battle was being called, in an effort to slow the German advance at least. As March arrived, Falkenhayn targeted the French positions on the left bank of the Meuse as well. Relentless attacks and bombardment continued throughout March, April and into May, but Falkenhayn made barely any progress. His only successes were in seeing off what amounted to suicidal counter-attacks by the recently appointed commander of the French sector, General Robert Nivelle (1856–1924). At the same time, there were fierce battles as the Germans captured French artillery on the Mort-Homme Ridge and Cote 304 to the west.

By June, the Germans were still making gains, but at a heavy cost. On 7 June, Fort Vaux fell after a desperate hand-to-hand fight inside its walls. The furthest point of the German advance was reached on 23 June when they were stopped in front of Fort Souville, the very last fortification before Verdun. When the Allies launched their offensive on the Somme on 1 July, the Germans could no longer keep attacking Verdun; their troops were needed at the Somme. The attack was abandoned and Falkenhayn had failed in his effort to bleed France to death.

But, the fighting at Verdun was not yet over. In October, the French counter-attacked, re-taking Fort Douaumont and Fort Vaux as well as 9,000 German captives. The 11-month Battle of Verdun had indeed been costly to the French with 542,000 casualties, but the Germans had also suffered with 434,000 casualties. The failure cost Falkenhayn his job; he was dismissed and replaced by Hindenburg and Ludendorff. On the Allied side, it might have been thought that Pétain would replace Joffre, but instead he was replaced by General Robert Nivelle who had commanded the French Second Army at Verdun and had led many of the bloody counter-offensives that had pushed the Germans back in late 1916.

There had already been changes in the British leadership. Towards the end of 1915, Field Marshal Sir John French – considered by many to be vain and arrogant – was replaced by Field Marshal Sir Douglas Haig (1861–1928) as Commander-in-Chief of the British armies on the Western Front. Haig was born into a famous Scotch whisky-distilling family and had served in the

Sudan and the Boer Wars. Deeply religious, he was considered more liberal and free-thinking than most senior officers. He had arrived in France in 1914 at the head of the British First Army and had distinguished himself in the defence of Ypres. He had never considered French suitable to command, an opinion he made clear to King George V in secret letters; his wife was a lady-in-waiting to the Queen. Whereas French hated trench warfare, Haig was supportive of the attritional nature of such a war, observing: 'The enemy should never be given a complete rest by day or night, but be relentlessly worn down by exhaustion and loss until his defence collapses'.

The Battle of the Somme

The new British commander might have preferred to delay any offensive until his new troops had a little more combat experience. He might also have wanted to delay matters until Britain's new secret weapon was available in sufficient quantities. An armoured fighting vehicle that ran on 'caterpillar' tracks and was capable of crossing trench lines was being developed. It was named the 'tank', a name chosen to maintain the secrecy of its development and eventual use, workers being led to believe, during construction, that they were merely building water tanks. Like Falkenhayn, however, Haig and the other senior officers knew that the most important element of that year's fighting would be the quantity of shells available.

The pressure that the French faced at Verdun through spring and early summer made it essential that the offensive on the Somme took place as soon as possible to divert the enemy's attention from its own offensive. It was planned to take place along a 17-mile front stretching from Gommecourt to just north of the

87

River Ancre and then southwards below Pozières Ridge and on to the Somme Valley. The main part of the offensive was to be undertaken by the French, with British troops of the Fourth Army of the BEF, commanded by General Sir Henry Rawlinson (1864–1925), supporting them on their northern flank. Haig planned for the overrunning of the German defences, allowing him to send cavalry through the resulting gap and to restore the war to one of movement, rather than the stasis of the last two years. On 24 June, the bombardment of the German trenches began, continuing for twenty-four hours a day for six days. Meanwhile, tunnellers were digging deep under the German lines, planting mines that were set to explode at the moment the offensive began. In the hours leading up to the signal for the men to go over the top, some of their officers are reported to have told them that the offensive would be easy, one even distributing footballs for his men to kick across no man's land and offering a prize to the first one to kick a ball into the enemy's trenches.

It turned out to be anything but easy and would, in fact, prove to be the most disastrous day in the illustrious history of the British army. As they made their way across no man's land, the troops discovered that the relentless bombardment by 1,000 field guns had failed to destroy the enemy barbed wire, many of the shells being defective and failing to explode. The nature of German trenches, dug deeper and better constructed than the British ones, had also ensured that many German soldiers had survived the bombardment. What's more, as soon as the shelling stopped, signalling the start of the advance, these German soldiers had been able to take up position behind their machine guns, ready for the British troops advancing slowly, line abreast as ordered by Rawlinson. The British were easy targets and soon their bodies were piled high in the clinging mud of no man's land. The British army sustained 57,000 casualties on that first day, a number that included 19,240 dead. All Haig had to show for this chilling loss of life was a small advance on the attack's right flank to a little way beyond the German front line. There was better news from the south, however, where the French overran the German first line and were advancing towards the second. The difference between the two attacks was that the French artillery was more effective, having employed more guns per mile of the front they were attacking than the British.

From that day until November, there is little evidence that Haig and Rawlinson were willing to revise their tactics and each wood, ridge and hamlet, changing hands repeatedly as the months passed, became the site of a battle that resulted in extraordinary numbers of casualties. Fighting for Mametz Wood, the 28th (Welsh) Division sustained 4,000 casualties; in a six-day battle to take Trones Wood, the 18th Division also suffered 4,000 casualties; only 773 of the 3,153 men of the South African Brigade that tried to drive the Germans out of Delville Wood were not wounded or killed; and 8,000 Australians died trying to take Pozières Ridge. Tanks were used in battle for the first time in heavy fighting around Flers. Of the 13 dispatched, 12 made it as far as the German lines and 6 advanced into the village.

By the end of the battle, twenty weeks after the initial bombardment, the Allies had succeeded in advancing seven miles but the desired breakthrough had not been made. Allied casualties were 614,105, British and Dominion troops making up 419,654 of those. The German cost was 650,000 casualties. Haig and Rawlinson have been heavily criticised for the human cost of the Battle of the Somme and for the failure to achieve very much in spite of the casualty toll and Winston Churchill was critical in cabinet, saying that this attritional type of warfare was more damaging to the British armies than to the German. Others have argued that the British generals had no other strategic option at the time and that the British losses should be compared with the millions lost by the Russians and the French already in the war.

What is certain, however, is that such huge loss of life affected not only the morale of fighting men, but also the view of the war on the home front. Recruitment figures fell noticeably, in spite of campaigns to boost the numbers, such as that of Lord Derby who recruited 300,000 men in autumn 1915. Finally, in January 1916, Prime Minister Asquith introduced conscription for all single men aged between 18 and 40. In April it was extended to include married men. Generally speaking, conscription, although objected to by a number of Liberal and Labour MPs as well as the trade unions, worked very efficiently and many considered it to be fair. Appeals against it on an individual basis were heard by tribunals and many factors such as family or health reasons could exempt a man from call-up. Tribunals also dealt with conscientious objectors but many were still sentenced to prison terms with hard labour while others worked in industry or in non-combatant roles in the armed forces.

The Eastern Front: the Brusilov Offensive

The campaign that the Russian High Command had agreed to mount was not welcomed by many of its commanders, following action they had undertaken at Vilna in Lithuania in March 1916. Unfortunately, their preparations for that action had been delayed and by the time they were ready to launch their offensive, the thaw had set in, everything being delayed in the resulting bad conditions underfoot. Their forces were vulnerable to counter-attack, leading to the offensive being aborted. Morale plummeted and commanders were of the opinion that it would be futile to try again until munitions had been sufficiently replenished. The catalyst for the summer offensive, timed to coincide with the action on the Western Front, was General Aleksei Brusilov (1853–1926), Commander of the South-western Front. He proposed that instead of his forces playing only a supporting role in the forthcoming action, they should attack at the same time as the planned offensive in the north. He also argued against the previous practice of attacking a small area of the front with a great density of firepower and manpower in order to achieve a breakthrough. This strategy, he argued, made it easy for the Central Powers' troops to counter-attack. Instead, he proposed, his forces should attack across the entirety of the South-western Front, confusing the enemy and hopefully causing them to collapse at one point. He would do it, he claimed, without seeking any increase in the materials and manpower at hand. Furthermore, he would not waste resources with the saturation shelling of areas of no strategic value. He would instead focus on command posts, roads and other important targets in an effort to disrupt the enemy's communications and weaken its command and control of the front.

Brusilov's strategy was put into action earlier than planned as the Italians were in dire need of help to the south. The Fifth Battle of Isonzo (9-15 March 1916) produced the same disappointing results as the previous four but plans by Italian commander Cadorna for another offensive were interrupted on 15 May by an Austro-Hungarian counter-offensive that targeted the Italian left flank at Trentino with the objective of breaking through and continuing to Venice. This would have been disastrous for the larger part of the Italian army on the Isonzo which would have been cut off and, if successful, it could have meant the end of the war for Italy. The offensive was supported by a massive artillery bombardment and Austrian commander-in-chief Conrad enjoyed some initial success. 400,000 Italians were taken prisoner as their defences crumbled and he came tantalisingly close to a breakthrough into the Venetian plain. It was at that point that the Italians turned to Brusilov for help in staging actions that would divert the Hapsburgs' attention away from their theatre. But, by the time Brusilov's troops swung into action, Conrad's momentum had diminished. The Russian troops began to have some astonishing impact on the south-eastern front, advancing 60 miles along the entire front in just one month and capturing 350,000 Hapsburg troops. His decision not to ask for additional supplies and manpower backfired on him, however, and he was unable to maintain the early successes. His force suffered from a paucity of reserves of men and weapons, while transport was also inadequate. When the Austro-Hungarian forces were bolstered by the arrival of German troops, Brusilov's advance ground to a halt. In late July the Russian High Command took the decision to launch its northern offensive against the Germans as agreed at Chantilly the previous December. Unfortunately, it faltered almost immediately as the Germans once again bettered them.

At this moment, with the army of Austria-Hungary in seemingly dire straits, Romania decided to enter the conflict on the side of the Allies who were as delighted by the news as the Central Powers were dismayed. The reward they were promised was support from the Allies for their objective of unifying all territories in which Romanians lived. But, the Romanians were no match for the Germans who, within months, had occupied almost two-thirds of their territory. Brusilov, so successful several months previously, was now caught up in Romania's ignominious defeat and, by the end of the year, all the ground that he had gained in his advance was once again under enemy control. Moreover, his armies had suffered a staggering 1.4 million casualties and were a spent force. It seemed even less likely following these actions that, despite their vast resources of men and materials, the Russians, would ever be able to come out on top against Germany.

The World at War: Mesopotamia

In 1914, a force of 10,000 British and Indian troops, commanded by Major General Sir Charles Townshend (1861–1924), had been sent to Mesopotamia – modern-day Iraq – to protect the oil installations at Abadan at the mouth of the Shatt-al-Arab strait and to prevent the Turks from threatening the Suez Canal. Townshend's force took the town of Kut-al-Amara, 497 miles upriver from Basra, at the head of the Persian Gulf, before making for Baghdad. After a year of defeats, the Turks had strengthened, however, and the Allied advance was halted by two days of tough fighting at the Battle of Ctesiphon. They retreated back to Kut where they were besieged for five awful months, from November 1915 to April 1916, by the German general, Colmar von der Goltz (1843–1916), known to the Ottomans as 'Goltz Pasha'. Goltz had been seconded to the Ottoman army by Germany before becoming military governor of invaded Belgium where he acted ruthlessly against the indigenous population. Now he was once again in the service of the Turks.

The besieged army suffered terribly in the dreadful heat of the day and malaria and dysentery were rife as medical supplies ran out. Food was also in short supply, leading to the slaughter of the army's 2,000 mules and 3,000 horses for meat. Indian troops, forbidden from eating meat by their religion, suffered even greater hardship. Meanwhile, the Turks launched three attacks on the town that were beaten back. Eventually, a truce was called so that talks could be held during which the Turks demanded unconditional surrender. Realising that it would be futile to keep resisting, Townshend ordered his troops to destroy everything in the town before raising the white flag of surrender. It was one of the worst defeats ever suffered by the British army and, coupled with the events of Gallipoli the previous year, did untold damage to British prestige and morale.

After enduring a forced march, the 13,000 survivors of the siege were treated brutally by their captors, 5,000 of them dying. This contrasted with the treatment of their commander. Townshend saw out the war in a comfortable villa on the shores of the Black Sea. Goltz Pasha died, supposedly of typhoid – although some say he was poisoned by the Turks – two weeks after the siege ended.

The Home Front

'There are only two divisions in the world today – human beings and Germans.' Thus did writer Rudyard Kipling (1865–1936) sum up the feelings of a people still burning with patriotic feeling and almost neurotic hatred of the enemy despite the slaughter on the battlefields of France. In Germany, that feeling was mirrored by such press statements as: 'The Englishman, indeed, is not to be classed among human beings.' Amongst soldiers, watching countless numbers of their comrades die, exhaustion and disillusionment were increasing while at home the public was being fed on propaganda reports that boasted of plucky victories and a despicable and dishonourable enemy. Publications such as Horatio Bottomley's (1860–1933) *John Bull* fuelled the fire of indignation at the Germans, dubbing them the 'Germ-hun'. This bestselling magazine became so popular during the war that one journalist wrote that 'next to Kitchener the most influential man today is Mr Horatio Bottomley'. Each side claimed that God was on its side. The Church of England vicar, Rev Basil Bourchier (1881–1933), captured by the Germans in Belgium, observed, for instance: 'This truly is a war of ideals; Odin is ranged against Christ, and Berlin is seeking to prove its supremacy over Bethlehem. Every shot that is fired, every bayonet thrust that gets home, every life that is sacrificed, is in very truth "for His Name's sake"'. On the German side a similar sentiment was embraced in the media: 'One thing is clear. God must stand on Germany's side. We fight for truth, culture and civilisation and human progress and true Christianity.'

As we have seen, unlike in past wars, the burden of this conflict was felt at home as well as on the battlefield, if only in terms of the huge numbers of families that suffered losses. Daily existence became increasingly harder as countries involved in the conflict devoted their national resources to winning the war. Blockades, too, began to take effect. German U-boats were becoming a particularly sharp thorn in the side of the British merchant fleet – tonnage of shipping sunk by them rose from 108,000 in July 1916 to 325,000 just four months later. Given that by this time Britain was dependent upon trade from overseas – principally the United States and Canada – for more than 60 per cent of her food, this was of particular concern. People began to have meatless days and coarser 'war bread' was introduced when there was a shortage of wheat in November 1916. Potatoes were often in short supply and individual consumption of sugar fell from 1.49 pounds in 1914 to 0.93 pounds in 1918.

In Germany, the Allied naval blockade had a huge impact on the day-to-day life of ordinary people as food shortages grew. They could no longer import food or critical goods such as farm fertiliser. Furthermore, the mistake of conscripting farm workers impacted hugely on food production. Food and clothing rationing was introduced in both Germany and Austria-Hungary. The food substitute – *ersatz* – became a staple, people drinking coffee made from roasted acorns, for example, and chemical substances taking the place of eggs and salad oil. Synthetic fabrics replaced wool and cotton, since textile factories had been converted to producing army uniforms. Coal was also in short supply. The winter of 1916–17 became known as the 'Turnip Winter' because people started using turnips, normally fed to livestock, as a substitute for potatoes and meat. That winter thousands of soup kitchens were opened, but hundreds of thousands died of illnesses related to hunger. Even soldiers' rations were cut. Tram services and street lighting were reduced while theatres and cabarets closed down.

Such strictures contributed to the weakening of the patriotic fervour of 1914 in both countries. In Britain, there were also internal problems. In 1914, Irish MPs in Parliament at Westminster had come out in support of Britain's war effort, but at Easter 1916 Irish nationalists rebelled in Dublin against British rule, a revolt that was crushed only after fierce street fighting. Russia, too, was beginning to feel the strain of the war effort at home. Russian industry had expanded rapidly to support the need for munitions and armaments. This had severely distorted the Russian economy and created more unrest than ever amongst the hungry subjects of the Tsar. Germany too, experienced unrest and there were strikes in Berlin and in the vital Ruhr coalfields. Food riots broke out and 30,000 marched in a peace demonstration in Frankfurt in October 1916. The French felt it possibly more than most, with a part of their territory occupied and millions of their young men killed on the battlefields. Many began to support the pacifist propaganda that was gaining ground. Indeed, peace was on the minds of many. In Britain, the pressure group, the Quaker-backed Union of Democratic Control was not strictly a pacifist movement, but had been working since 1914 to remove military influence from the government. It called for a full examination of war aims and opposed conscription and wartime censorship. Some such as Lord Lansdowne, himself a member of the War Cabinet, wondered if eventual victory was worth the slaughter of millions of young men.

On December 12, the German government, basking in the glow of victory in Romania, instigated the first official peace initiative of the war. It was, however, tactless and arrogant, talking of the 'gigantic advantages' that Germany had gained in the field and boasting of further anticipated successes. The terms of the peace as promulgated by Chancellor Bethmann Hollweg included German control of Poland and Belgium and France would have to cede to Germany the industrial iron-ore rich area of Longwy-Briey in the centre of the Lorraine mining district. For the Allies, even though exhausted, these demands were wholly unacceptable, especially in view of the sacrifices and losses to date, but particularly as the efforts of their industries were at last beginning to bear fruit. Huge quantities of munitions and aircraft were finally being sent to the front.

5

1917
The Beginning of the End

Lines of grey, muttering faces, masked with fear,
They leave their trenches, going over the top,
While time ticks blank and busy on their wrists,
And hope, with furtive eyes and grappling fists,
Flounders in the mud. O Jesus, make it stop!
From 'Attack', by Siegfried Sassoon

Germany Goes on the Defensive

As 1917 arrived, it was time for a reappraisal. The previous year had brought contrasting fortunes for the Kaiser's troops on the Eastern and Western Fronts but it was hoped that the introduction of fresh blood at the top – Hindenburg and Ludendorff – would give fresh impetus to the German forces in both theatres. The German war economy and the German army had been put under considerable strain in 1916, with the entry of Romania into the war and the Germans had been forced to devote more troops to the Eastern Front. The two new commanders, however, did not envisage much action in the east in the coming months, since the Russians had taken such a beating in 1916. They also quickly concluded that the tactics of 1916 – wearing down the enemy with relentless offensives as at Verdun – were a non-starter for this year. Instead, they would go on the defensive while the army recovered, even ceding territory if necessary. In September 1916, work had begun on the construction of the *Siegfriedstellung* (Hindenburg

Line), a shorter defensive position behind the Noyon Salient. It was intended to counter an Allied breakthrough and to offer prepared positions to which a retreating German army could withdraw. It would also take fewer troops to defend it as it provided a shorter front. Meanwhile, the zone in front of this position was to be destroyed; bridges, railway lines and roads would be blown up, meaning that it would take weeks for the Allies to progress towards the Hindenburg Line. Troops had been transferred from the east, raising the number of divisions to 133 at the end of January 1917, but this was still not enough. Meanwhile, there was a shortfall in the production of explosives, ammunition and weapons with only an estimated 60 per cent of the target expected to be achieved by the summer of 1917. The withdrawals from territory that so many German soldiers had died for took place in February and April, after the British had forced the German First Army back on the Somme front in the first two months of the year. As they went, they destroyed the infrastructure and many buildings, leaving homeless civilians behind in terrible conditions, news of which brought further disgrace to Germany's reputation.

Hindenburg and Ludendorff launched a programme of extensive industrial mobilisation in Germany, the entire German economy being harnessed for the war effort. But they also focused on a campaign at sea that they hoped would force Britain into submission. Their fleet of U-boats would target merchant shipping, both Allied and neutral.

The Allies: More of the Same

Meanwhile, the Entente Powers returned to tactics that had already been tried on the Eastern Front and which, unfortunately, had failed. In the east, they planned offensives in the north and south, even though the Russian army had taken a terrible battering in the past two years and was hardly in the best condition. Perhaps they believed that putting Brusilov in charge would make it different this time. In the west, new commander Robert Nivelle carried the hopes of all, having led a number of successful counter-attacks during the latter stages of the Battle of Verdun. But there was change, too, in the government of Britain. The Liberal politician David Lloyd George had become Secretary of State for War in June 1916, but, frustrated by the limitations of his role, launched a campaign with the support of Lord Northcliffe (1865–1922), proprietor of the *Daily Mail* and the *Daily Mirror*, to be installed at the head of a small committee that would manage the war effort. Asquith at first acquiesced, on condition that he be kept informed and allowed to attend meetings whenever he wanted. But, a *Times* editorial which suggested he was being sidelined made him withdraw his consent to Lloyd George's chairmanship of the committee. Asquith would instead be chairman. Lloyd George reacted angrily to the news, resigning from the committee immediately, but it soon became evident that support for the Prime Minister was declining, both in the press and amongst leading Conservatives. On 5 December 1916, he finally resigned, adding that he would not serve under any other Prime Minister. Two days later, David Lloyd George became Prime Minister and head of the coalition government. He immediately formed the much more compact War Cabinet that he had earlier proposed.

The new Prime Minister was keen to see the war to its bitter conclusion – a fight to a finish or 'to a knockout', as he described it. He did not get on with Haig, however, and was determined that there would be no repeat of the bloodletting of 1916. To this end, he devised a plan by which Italy would play a major role in the coming year. Unsurprisingly, the Italians were reluctant to be the year's sacrificial victims and the plan was consigned to the wastebasket. Instead, Lloyd George reluctantly accepted Nivelle's plan for a French offensive on the Chemin des Dames in the spring that the general rather optimistically believed would deliver an Allied victory. The offensive would be supported to the north by a British attack at Arras. Remarkably, Lloyd George agreed to Nivelle taking command of the British forces during this offensive rather than Haig, a decision that drove a wedge between the Prime Minister and British army headquarters for the duration of the war.

The Threat from Beneath the Waves

It was a risky decision to launch a campaign of unrestricted submarine warfare as the Germans did early in 1917, mainly because it was almost inevitable that it would result in the United States, with its wealth of resources and manpower, entering the war on the Allied side. Up until this time, the Americans had had little stomach for war and, at the end of 1916, President Woodrow Wilson had already attempted to intervene as a peacemaker, writing to each side asking it to state its demands. In January 1917, the Germans rebuffed his request, seeking instead 'a direct exchange of views'. The Allied governments, on the other hand, presented clear demands that sought the evacuation of occupied territories, reparations to be made to France, Russia and Romania and recognition by the Central Powers of the principle of nationalities. This would include the liberation of Italians, Slavs, Romanians, Czecho-Slovaks, and the establishment of a 'free and united Poland'. They demanded guarantees preventing or limiting wars in the future, as a condition of any peace settlement. The attempt failed and the Allies refused to enter into any negotiations until all occupied territories were evacuated and indemnities were paid for damage done.

Certain that there would be no decisive victory on the Western Front in 1917, the German High Command once again turned to their submarines – U-boats – which they hoped would sever the British lifeline from the United States. The British had been the largest foreign investor in American business and those investments were now being cashed in and exchanged for vital supplies of food and war materials. Of course, international law forbade the sinking without warning of civilian ships, especially as they might be neutral and might not even be carrying cargos of war materials. Most Germans, however, cared little for such quibbles. They were starving, after all, and the Americans were going out of their way to be helpful to the British, to the extent of providing loans to them that helped maintain the value of sterling whilst also providing France with the means to keep going. What would be the difference, some Germans argued, if the Americans did enter the war?

Earlier in the conflict, the Germans did not have enough submarines, but in 1916, 108 were built and a pen for lighter vessels was constructed at Zeebrugge in Belgium. From there, they could launch attacks on ships transporting goods and troops across the Channel. Admiral Henning von Holtzendorff (1853–1919), head of the German Navy General Staff, drafted a memo about unrestricted submarine warfare to the Kaiser in December 1916, claiming his submarines could sink 600,000 tons of shipping every month, causing untold damage to the British economy and to British food supplies. On 1 February 1917, against the wishes of German Chancellor Bethmann Hollweg, a zone around western France and the British Isles was declared open to sinking on sight. The United States and a number of South American countries, including Brazil, Peru and Bolivia, immediately severed diplomatic relations with Germany. In February, 540,000 tons were sunk and in March almost the 600,000 that Holtzendorff had promised. In April, his estimate was exceeded with the sinking of 881,000 tons, 545,000 of which were British. The ships were generally hit as they bunched together shortly before arriving in port, and the result was the withdrawal of neutral vessels, ships being laid up and many American citizens losing their lives.

To defend shipping against the underwater threat, a hydrophone was invented that could detect sound beneath the surface and depth charges were developed and carried by destroyers. The eventual solution, however, was the convoy system, a group of merchant ships sailing together with a protective naval escort. In the first three months of the convoys, from May to July, of 8,894 ships convoyed, only 27 were sunk by U-boats. Furthermore, U-boat losses rose, 15 being sunk in the same period around British waters, compared to 9 the previous quarter. Unrestricted submarine warfare had failed to inflict the promised damage on the British economy.

Beleaguered Russia

The Russian campaign planned for 1 May 1917 failed to materialise. The build-up had begun and, by early March, 62 divisions and a great deal of firepower had been assembled. But it had become obvious earlier in the year that Russian resolve was crumbling. The transport system was in a state of collapse and the morale of the Russian army was at rock bottom, desertions approaching a staggering two million. Meanwhile, at home, the economic situation was out of control and there was increasing talk of a revolution to replace the Tsar who had become so hated that even many of his erstwhile supporters wanted him to go. The war had brought a wave of patriotic feeling in Russia and, during the first months, the Tsar had enjoyed the support of his people. By 1917, however, the toll the fighting had taken on the economy and on the Russian population had turned this support into loathing, exacerbated by escalating food prices and fuel shortages. Radical political groups such as the Populists, the Octobrists and the Social Revolutionaries had long talked of revolution. Another group, the Social Democrats dedicated their movement to following the communist theories devised by the German philosopher, sociologist and economist Karl Marx (1818–1883) but, amidst factional fighting in 1903, had split into two groups – the Mensheviks and the Bolsheviks. The Bolsheviks were led by Vladimir Ulyanov (1870–1924), better known as Lenin.

The revolution began in February in Petrograd (now St Petersburg) in response to food shortages. There were strikes and mass demonstrations, leading to armed clashes with the police. Soon, disaffected troops from the city's garrison began to side with the revolutionaries. Eventually, on 15 March, Tsar Nicholas II, his support gone, even amongst the military, was left with no choice but to abdicate, bringing to an end the Romanov Dynasty that had ruled Russia for more than three hundred years. The Tsar was replaced by a Provisional Government, made up of liberals and socialists, led by Prince Georgy Lvov (1861–1925) that promised elections and democracy. While this was happening, the Germans made no moves on the Eastern Front to take advantage of the Russian preoccupation with internal matters, believing that the new regime would seek peace. Pressured by France and Britain, however, the new government agreed to remain committed to the war.

The Provisional Government shared power with the influential

Petrograd Soviet, a workers' council that ordered all Russian soldiers to obey only its orders and the Russian army began to dismantle. Lenin, at the time exiled in Switzerland, set out for Russia as soon as he could, his journey facilitated by the Germans who allowed him passage through Germany in a sealed train carriage and provided financial support. It would be advantageous to Germany, after all, if revolutionary unrest were to spread in Russia. With the slogan 'Peace, bread and land', Lenin demanded an end to Russian involvement in the war and for power to be handed to the soviets. The country was in turmoil for weeks, news of further defeats on the battlefield fomenting even greater unrest. Accused by the Provisional Government, now led by the moderate socialist Alexander Kerensky (1881–1970), of being in the pay of the Germans, Lenin was forced to flee to Finland. But, Kerensky's leadership was almost immediately challenged when General Lavr Kornilov (1870–1918) and other military leaders, supported by businessmen and industrialists, tried to seize control. Kerensky made the mistake of asking the Bolsheviks for help but Lenin, now back in Petrograd, had only one aim – to seize power for himself and his party. The October Revolution, launched on 24–25 of that month, was met with little opposition. In November, Lenin ordered Russian troops to stop fighting and announced that he was willing to enter negotiations with Germany. The two sides met at Brest-Litovsk, but when the Russian representative, Leon Trotsky (1879–1940), refused to accept Germany's terms, the Germans responded by resuming their advance on Petrograd. Lenin ordered Trotsky to accept the terms, regardless of how harsh they were.

The Allies were, of course, crestfallen, but Germany was also a loser as a result of the Russian Revolution. At the end of the war on the Eastern Front, many German troops returned home, their heads filled with revolutionary ideas. The influence of these ideas would be felt during the closing months of the war the following year.

The Nivelle Offensive

As Russia fell apart, the Allies watched anxiously, thankful that their political institutions were strong enough to avoid a similar collapse, despite the setbacks of the previous year, the stalled offensives and the huge loss of life. In April 1917, Nivelle's offensive on the Chemin des Dames was launched with initial success in the first four days of the month, the French capturing German defences west of the Hindenburg Line near St Quentin. Further attacks were repelled, however. Meanwhile, the offensive by the British First and Third armies was the only part of the campaign to gain any real advantage, taking Vimy Ridge with Canadian support and achieving the greatest advance in a single day of the war on the Western Front so far. They also inflicted a large number of casualties on the enemy. Ultimately, however, the British attempt to break through ended in failure and at great cost, like the efforts of the previous year. Despite this, the earlier British success suggested that the industrial might of Britain and her dominions was beginning to have a bearing on the war. Nonetheless, the desired breakthrough was not forthcoming – the cavalry was again inadequate and the artillery, effective though it was, was not mobile enough to push home the advantage.

On 16 April, the French launched their main offensive on the Aisne, Nivelle promising a breakthrough within forty-eight hours. But the Germans simply retreated to reverse-facing slopes and defended in depth. In the end, for all Nivelle's promised innovations, it seemed little different from Joffre's efforts of 1916 and by 25 April it had stalled. The reaction amongst politicians and soldiers – both rank-and-file and commanding officers – was one of revulsion and disappointment. Casualties and losses on the Allied side were 163,000 while the Germans lost 187,000, including 29,000 dead. The French President and members of his government were warned by lower ranking officers that nothing would come of a continuation of operations in this way and Nivelle was replaced by the saviour of Verdun – Philippe Pétain.

Pétain faced a grave situation following the failure at Chemin des Dames. There was great unrest amongst French troops and this disaffection led to mutinies in 68 of the French army's 112 divisions. Soldiers engaged in spontaneous acts of 'collective disobedience'. Those at the top condemned these acts as the work of revolutionaries and agitators but it was obvious that the conduct of the war had to change. Pétain eased the situation by exercising commendable caution in dealing with the unrest. He restricted the executions of mutineers to fifty or seventy, a small number given the serious nature of the mutinies. He also improved soldiers' conditions, giving them better food and shelters and providing more opportunities for them to visit their families at home. He further promised that French lives would no longer be squandered the way they had been in the first years of the war. From then until the arrival of the Americans and the introduction of the revolutionary new Renault FT–17 tank in May 1918, the French held the line but did not mount any further major offensives.

In the absence of the French in the second half of 1917, it was left to the British to launch major operations against the Germans.

The United States Enters the War

On 2 April 1917, President Wilson spoke to the US Congress on Washington's Capitol Hill, asking them to declare war on Germany:

> 'To such a task we can dedicate our lives and our fortunes, everything that we are and everything we have, with the pride of those who know that the day has come when America is privileged to spend her blood and her might for the principles that gave her birth and happiness and the peace which she has treasured. God helping her, she can do no other'

Wilson had pursued a policy of neutrality since the outbreak of war, while also working hard to broker a peace agreement. It was a long-standing desire of the United States never to become involved in a European war but eventually that view was no longer tenable. America had been enraged by the deaths of 128 of her citizens in the sinking of the *Lusitania* in 1915. However, while demanding an end to indiscriminate attacks on passenger shipping at the time, Wilson had urged Americans to turn the other cheek. It was a sentiment that did not go down at all well in Britain, but Germany did comply with his demand that unrestricted attacks end. In 1916, Wilson was narrowly re-elected president, partly because many Americans were pleased that he had kept them out of the war.

When Germany resumed unrestricted submarine warfare in January 1917, it did so knowing that it would almost certainly bring America into the conflict. Shortly after, there was a critical diplomatic incident that hardened the hearts of the American public against the Germans, if, indeed, any further hardening was needed. On 16 January, the German Foreign Secretary, Arthur Zimmermann (1864–1940), sent a coded telegram to the German ambassador to Mexico, Heinrich von Eckardt, instructing him that if the United States appeared to be ready to declare war on Germany, he should approach the Mexican government to propose a military alliance. In return, Germany would guarantee the restoration to Mexico of territories in Texas, New Mexico and Arizona that had been lost to the United States in 1836 and 1848. The telegram also asked Eckardt to broker an alliance between Germany and Japan. The Mexicans simply ignored the proposal but the telegram fell into Allied hands and, using captured cypher documents, was deciphered by British code-breaker, Nigel de Grey (1886–1951). The British were reluctant to release the text of the telegram to the Americans because it would disclose the fact that they had access to German codes. Pretending to have received it by other means, the British passed the telegram to the secretary of the US embassy in Berlin from where its contents were conveyed to President Wilson. There was incredulity at first, but Arthur Zimmermann himself confirmed the truth of the story at a press conference in March.

Meanwhile, unrestricted submarine warfare was resumed, leading to the sinking of seven American ships. This brought a wave of anti-German sentiment across the United States, feelings that were only heightened by the Zimmermann telegram which was seen as a *casus belli*, a cause for war. Wilson tried to win over anti-war elements by explaining that, if the Allies won this war, it would mean an end to all wars. Anyway, he also argued, it would be beneficial to America to have a voice at the peace conference. On 6 April 1917, the United States Congress declared war on Germany.

The United States Army was small, but the Selective Service

Act was enacted on 17 May, authorising the federal government to raise a national army through conscription. It took some time to do all this but 2.8 million men were drafted and, by the summer of 1918, America was sending 10,000 fresh troops to France every day. A battleship group was sent to Scapa Flow to meet up with the British Grand Fleet, destroyers were dispatched to Queenstown in Ireland and submarines were provided to help guard convoys.

From this moment on, there could really be only one conclusion to the war.

The Third Battle of Ypres (Passchendaele)

After Nivelle's failure, the British army would no longer be under French command. In fact, Haig seemed to be the only Allied commander that year who had improved his reputation. Lloyd George had certainly not improved his as a leader of British strategy in the war but Haig's desire to launch a major campaign in Belgium that would result in British forces pushing out from the Ypres Salient to the coast seemed an unlikely option to be taken up by the politicians. Campaigns with large strategic aims had failed up until now, as demonstrated by the offensives of 1915, 1916 and by Nivelle's initiative earlier in the year. Political leaders appeared to be more of the opinion that offensives with limited aspirations – attacks that remained within the range of artillery – were likely to reap greater rewards. In considering actions of this kind, they were also mindful of how close French troops had come to outright mutiny and were keen not to push their men too far. Despite all this, however, Haig's plan was endorsed by the politicians.

The plan was to seek control of the ridges south and east of the Belgian city of Ypres in West Flanders. Passchendaele was a village situated on the last ridge to the east of Ypres and it was five miles from a crucial part of the German Fourth Army's supply system, the railway station at Roeselare. British forces would then advance to Torhout-Couckelaere where they would shut down the rail link that ran through Roeselare and Torhout. Meanwhile, an attack was planned along the Belgian coast from Nieuwpoort, pushing forward to Bruges and then the Dutch border. Before the offensive started, Haig needed to capture the Messines Ridge, near the village of Messines in West Flanders, in order to prevent the Germans from observing his preparations from it. Its capture would also give the Allies control of a strategically important area on the southern flank of the Ypres Salient, would shorten the front and would allow the British a good vantage point from which to observe the southern slope of the Menin Ridge while they were getting ready for the offensive in the Ypres Salient.

The Battle of Messines began on 7 June with the detonation of nineteen large mines, containing a million tons of TNT, that British tunnellers had been placing under German positions on the ridge since 1915. At the same time, a huge artillery bombardment was unleashed on German batteries. The ridge was taken with only moderate casualties being incurred but Haig then paused, to allow General Sir Hubert Gough (1870–1963) to take command of the main offensive, a hiatus that allowed the Germans to regroup in the Ypres Salient and strengthen their defences. The attack started with an enormous artillery bombardment that allowed the infantry to make some advances. In the area of the crucial Gheluvelt Plateau, however, little progress was made. It was essential that this plateau was taken in order to facilitate further advances on the Passchendaele Ridge and onwards to the Belgian coast. Conditions became appalling as heavy rain fell on the battlefield throughout August, holding up operations and causing sickness amongst the troops. Haig shuffled his commanders at this point, moving Gough to the flanks and putting General Herbert Plumer (1857–1932) in charge of the main offensive. Plumer made lengthy preparations but his ambition was limited and, although in late September and early October he carried out three successful attacks (Polygon Wood, Menin Road and Broodseinde), the results were limited. The tactics involved artillery barrages, although not as great as those available to Gough, being fired in front of the advancing troops. On arriving at their objective, the soldiers were given cover from counter-offensives by further barrages. The amount of ground gained by these actions was small, limited to little more than 3,000 yards. After the third attack, the heavy rain returned to the battlefield and conditions once again became intolerable. At this point, the artillery became less effective, rendering Plumer's tactics useless, but the offensive was not halted and the struggle began for Passchendaele Ridge, a prize that now had little strategic value. Artillery support could not be moved up because of the conditions whilst Allied troops were, by this time, exhausted and morale was low. Finally, a modest British advance in the land opposite Passchendaele was lost after German counter-attacks. The cost was 13,000 Allied troops, including 2,735 New Zealanders of whom 845 were either dead or stranded beyond help in the quagmire that was the battlefield. Haig and his commanders finally agreed at a conference on 13 October to halt operations until the weather showed some signs of improvement. Meanwhile, communications would be improved so that supplies and munitions could be transported to the front.

It was an episode from which no one – neither politicians nor military commanders – could take any satisfaction. There were 275,000 British casualties of whom 70,000 were dead or missing. To make matters worse, all the ground gained in the Ypres offensive was re-captured by the Germans in just three days in 1918 when the Allies had to retreat from the area. As Lloyd George later wrote in his memoirs: 'Passchendaele was indeed one of the greatest disasters of the war... No soldier of any intelligence now defends this senseless campaign...'

The Battle of Cambrai

The huge loss of life at Ypres did not deflect Haig and the politicians back in London from their desire to maintain the pressure on the Germans. Added to this was Haig's wish to redeem himself following the disasters of the previous months. It had been observed that, in a relatively quiet sector of the Western Front, near Cambrai in the Nord department of northern France, the Germans did not have a very large force guarding the line. Cambrai was an important supply point for the Hindenburg Line and the seizure of the Bourlon Ridge nearby would enable the Allies to present a threat to the rear of the German line to the north. Importantly, the ground had not been subjected to relentless artillery bombardments and that would at last offer an opportunity to employ a large force of tanks as raiding parties. There would be 434 of them in this battle. Additionally, new innovative artillery techniques were introduced, sound rangers locating the enemy guns sufficiently accurately for them to be pinpointed on a map and targeted. A consequence of this was an additional element of surprise, as the gunners no longer had to rely on watching where shells fell in order to improve their aim. Therefore, the bombardment could commence simultaneously with the advance of tanks and infantry.

The battle began at dawn on 20 November and the combination of surprise, the accuracy of the artillery and the use of large numbers of tanks proved successful, the Germans fleeing as tanks smashed through their defences, closely followed by infantry. They rushed in reserves and began to shore up the line, stopping the British who lacked sufficient support to make a decisive breakthrough. Soon, German stormtroopers (*Sturmtruppen*) began to break through the British line, managing to drive Haig's men back to their starting-point. In the battle, 65 tanks were destroyed by the Germans, 73 broke down and 43 got stuck in the mud, rendering the first major use of tanks in battle no more than a qualified success. 11,500 German prisoners were taken and the attack persuaded the Allies that it was possible to breach the Hindenburg Line and demonstrated the value of the new artillery and infantry tactics. Later in the war, these would prove even more invaluable.

Disaster for the Italians on the South-eastern Front

The Italian leaders were content to maintain operations against the Austro-Hungarians but were unwilling to take on the much more daunting might of the Germans, happy to allow the French and the British to deal with them. Battles at Isonzo – the tenth and eleventh battles of the conflict on that river – had rewarded them with minimal advance at great cost, with General Cadorna's troops poorly trained and lacking not only battle experience, but also modern weapons and transport. That may have been partly the cause of Cadorna's insistence by the autumn of 1917 that he would not be launching any further attacks that year, news that dismayed the other members of the Entente. In October, however, having resisted the British in Belgium, the Germans diverted troops to Italy to reinforce the Hapsburg forces. Hindenburg had concluded that in order to keep the Austro-Hungarians in the war, the Italians had to be dealt a severe beating. Ludendorff was not convinced of the wisdom of this strategy but he was overruled. Following reconnaissance of the Isonzo front as to where would be the most suitable location for a gas attack, the quiet Caporetto area was selected and a new 14th Army was assembled using nine Austrian and six German divisions, commanded by General Otto von Below (1857–1944).

The Battle of Caporetto – also known as the 12th Battle of the Isonzo – that began on 24 October, was an unmitigated disaster for the Italians who lost all the territory they had gained in the last thirty months of fighting, gains that had cost a third of a million Italian lives. When the Germans broke through the Italian lines, Cadorna's troops fled, deserters blocking the roads on their way home to the extent that reserves could not make their way through them to the front. Cadorna had little option but to order a retreat, his troops falling back a distance of some 59 miles. At that point, a stand was made and the offensive was finally halted but not before Italy had incurred 40,000 casualties and suffered a significant humiliation. British and French troops were hurriedly dispatched to reinforce their lines. The Italian government, meanwhile, sought to place the blame on left-wing agitators and defeatist attitudes. Cadorna's role came under close scrutiny, of course, and he was replaced by General Armando Diaz (1861–1928).

The Middle East

Following General Townshend's debacle at Kut, there were demands from politicians such as Lord Curzon (1859–1925) and Austen Chamberlain (1863–1937) for further advances in Mesopotamia in order to restore British prestige in the Middle East. This was manifestly against the wishes of the Chief of the General Staff, Field Marshal Sir William Robertson (1860–1933). Nonetheless, a new commander was appointed, Lieutenant General Sir Frederick Maude (1864–1917) who was dispatched with three extra divisions of mixed British and Indian troops to the region. Maude's tactics were to advance only over small areas and to do so only if backed by artillery. In this manner, his force advanced steadily along the River Tigris, winning at Mohammed Abdul Hassan, Hai and Dahra in January 1917 and on 24 February, Kut was re-captured. Turkish resistance crumbled and, two weeks later, Maude entered Baghdad from where he launched the Samarrah Offensive while continuing operations on the Euphrates and Diyala rivers. The total British losses in the campaign were around 90,000 men, including Lieutenant General Maude himself who died of cholera in November 1917 after drinking milk that had not been boiled.

Meanwhile, the campaign in Sinai and Palestine continued. General Sir Archibald Murray (1860–1945), commander-in-chief of Egypt, decided in 1916 that the best way to protect the Suez Canal would be for the Egyptian Expeditionary Force (EEF) to occupy the Sinai Peninsula. The Anzac Mounted Division and the 52nd (Lowland) Division forced the Ottomans to retreat from the region, defeating them at the Battle of Romani in August. Murray waited for several months while a water pipeline and railway were built across the desert with which he could supply his forces as they advanced. Resuming hostilities, the EEF defeated the Ottomans again at the Battle of Magdhaba in December. That month a new army corps known as the Desert Column was created, completing the re-capture of Sinai at the Battle of Rafa on 9 January 1917. Substantial amounts of Egyptian territory were recaptured by this campaign but Murray, determined to capture Gaza and force a Turkish retreat from Palestine, did not stop there. In March and April, however, the EEF suffered defeats in the First and Second Battles of Gaza, with a loss of 6,500 casualties. It was a bad time to lose as it coincided with the failure of the Nivelle Offensive in France, unrest amongst Russian troops after the February Revolution and the resumption of unrestricted submarine warfare by the Germans. Murray was relieved of his command and replaced by General Sir Edmund Allenby (1861–1936).

From April until October, there was a stalemate in southern Palestine. Troops were brought in from the Western Front and Allenby, now in charge of seven British infantry divisions and three cavalry divisions, had orders to take Jerusalem. He defeated the Turks at Beersheba, Tel el Khuweilfe, Hareira and Sheiria and Gaza and forced the Ottoman army into a retreat. On 9 October, he entered Jerusalem, making sure to walk in instead of riding and going bareheaded, as a deliberate contrast with what was viewed as the arrogant entry into the city of the Kaiser on horseback in 1898.

Throughout this campaign, the Turks had been forced to send troops and equipment to the Hejaz, a region in the west of modern-day Saudi Arabia to try to suppress an Arab revolt that had broken out after Sharif Hussein bin Ali (1854–1931) had proclaimed himself king of an independent Hejaz. The revolt was supported by British money, weapons and resources and a representative of the British Foreign Office's Arab Bureau, TE Lawrence (1888–1935), who has since become famous, of course, as 'Lawrence of Arabia'. Lawrence had travelled extensively within the Levant and Mesopotamia before the war and was recruited by the Arab Bureau which had devised a campaign to support local tribes against the Ottomans, forcing them to divert their forces to that area, weakening their positions elsewhere. Lawrence had been working with the Hashemite Arabs in the Hejaz since October 1916, fighting in guerrilla operations alongside Arab irregular forces commanded by Emir Faisal (1885–1933), son of Sharif Hussein. The strategy was effective and large numbers of Turkish troops were tied down in this area.

1917: In Conclusion

Germany had started 1917 believing that it would be a year of remaining on the defensive while building up its resources. It had achieved a great deal more, however. One of its enemies, Russia, had been eliminated and another, Italy, had suffered a shattering defeat at Caporetto. The resource-sapping war on two fronts could be a thing of the past. In the west, on the other hand, the defensive nature of the year had used up both men and resources and the one attempt at gaining victory had been defeated. Meanwhile, the submarine campaign had brought disaster; it had failed to knock Britain out of the war and worse still, it had finally persuaded the Americans to eschew neutrality and dedicate their massive resources to the Allied effort.

Thus, the Allies ended the year with high hopes. Not only did they now have the Americans fighting alongside them, they had a tremendous array of weaponry at their disposal, Britain having successfully mobilised her industry to make an even greater contribution to the war effort. Of course, the squandering of British lives in 1917 has to be recognised as a considerable negative, especially in view of the German offensives that were to come in 1918.

6

1918
Endgame

I have a rendezvous with Death
At some disputed barricade,
When Spring comes back with rustling shade
And apple-blossoms fill the air—
From 'I Have a Rendezvous with Death', by Alan Seeger

The Home Front: Rationing

The U-boat campaign had failed, but nonetheless, as a consequence of it, rationing was finally introduced in Britain. At the start of the war, there had been an outbreak of panic-buying of food items, people hoarding them at home. Some shops were cleared out in just days after the outbreak of war. Things soon returned to normal, however. The Defence of the Realm Act had tried to prevent hoarding and gave the authorities the right to take over any land not being used for food production in order to grow crops on it. The government converted more than 2.5 million acres of land to food production, the work being done by the Women's Land Army as most farm labourers had been called up to fight. Despite women's contributions to the war effort, however, notions of female behaviour were still entrenched in some quarters. A government message to the women thus employed read:

'You are doing a man's work and so you are dressed rather like a man; but remember that because you wear a smock and trousers you should take care to behave like an English girl who expects chivalry and respect from everyone she meets.'

Meanwhile, people turned their gardens into allotments and kept chickens in their back gardens. But it was still not enough and the government attempted to introduce a voluntary code of rationing whereby people established their own restrictions on what they ate, with the Royal Family spearheading the campaign. This, too, enjoyed limited success and with prices soaring, there was a rising tide of resentment that workers in the all-important munitions factories were unable to afford enough food while those with money could buy more than they required on the black market.

When the campaign of unrestricted submarine warfare was launched by the Germans in early 1917, there was a dramatic impact on Britain's imports of food from her main suppliers, Canada and the United States. By April 1917, Britain had only six weeks of wheat left and, of course, bread was a staple item of most people's diet. Malnutrition in poorer communities became a concern, leading the government to finally introduce food rationing in January 1918, at first in the Home Counties and the South East and then across the rest of the country. As the year went on, different food products were added to the growing list of rationed items. In January, sugar was rationed and by the end of April, meat, cheese, butter and margarine had been added to the list. The government issued ration-cards and people had to register with a butcher and a grocer, each person being allowed 15 ounces of meat, 5 ounces of bacon and 4 ounces of butter or margarine a week. It was effective. The problems of rising prices and food queues were solved and malnutrition disappeared. Some suggest that people's health actually improved as a result of rationing; the poor received a better share of the available food and the well off ate less.

President Wilson's Fourteen Points

On 8 January 1918, President Wilson delivered a speech presenting a list of terms for a peace agreement that was called the Fourteen Points. Wilson demanded transparency in peace negotiations; freedom of navigation on the open seas in peace and in war; the removal of economic barriers and equality of trade amongst all nations agreeing to the peace; guarantees concerning the reduction of armaments; free and impartial decisions on colonial claims, taking into consideration the interests of the peoples in question; the evacuation of all Russian, French (including Alsace-Lorraine), Belgian, Romanian, Serbian and Montenegrin territory; a readjustment of Italy's borders along clearly recognisable lines of nationality; autonomous development for the peoples of Austria-Hungary; autonomous development for nationalities under Ottoman rule; the creation of an independent Polish state; and the establishment of a general association of nations.

None of America's allies was aware he was going to make such a speech and it was not well received by all. French Prime Minister Georges Clemenceau (1841–1929), on hearing about the Fourteen Points, is reported to have exclaimed, *'Le bon Dieu n'en avait que dix!'* (The good Lord only had ten!). The French and Italians accepted them on 1 November and Britain later agreed to all the points apart from the one regarding the freedom of the seas. Furthermore, Britain wanted to force Germany to pay reparations and to have that added to the list of points. The speech was used as propaganda by the Allies, copies of it being widely distributed in Germany and dropped behind the German lines before the end of the war, with the intention of making the Germans believe that if they surrendered the ensuing settlement would be just. It should be pointed out that the Fourteen Points had little to do with the Treaty of Versailles negotiated in 1919 and, indeed, the United States never ratified the treaty.

Germany Remains Optimistic

Despite huge campaigns such as those fought at Verdun, Ypres and the Somme, nothing had matched the intensity of the battles that had taken place during the first few months of the war. In the first three weeks of fighting, for instance, Britain lost 330,000 men, killed or captured, about a sixth of the total number of British casualties in the entire war. That intensity returned, however, in the first six months of 1918. At last Ludendorff had the resources to start winning, with a good supply of weapons and munitions at his disposal. In the closing months of the war, from July to November, when the Allies had the upper hand, the numbers involved climbed rapidly. Both sides were also supported by quantities of weapons and munitions that could only be dreamed of in 1914. Of course, as the numbers involved in the fighting rose, so too did the casualties.

Remarkably, given that the submarine campaign had ultimately been a failure and that America was now fighting on the opposite side, the Germans began 1918 in buoyant mood. The Americans, after all, would take some time to gear up for war and the British were exhausted following their efforts at Cambrai and in Flanders the previous year. The French would be incapable of anything until at least the summer and Russia was no longer a combatant. All the troops on the Eastern Front were now available to Ludendorff and

Hindenburg and with another 100,000 workers conscripted into the army from industry at home, Germany was, momentarily at any rate, numerically superior on the Western Front where her 192 divisions faced the Allies' 169. Ludendorff was determined to exploit this advantage to the full, planning to go on the offensive for the spring of 1918.

His principal target was the British army, because it was evident that, until Britain was defeated, the war could not be won. He chose the area between Arras and St Quentin as the location for his attack, hoping that he might separate the French and British Armies and push the British into the sea. He would concentrate all his forces there, including the troops that had been brought in from the east, a total of around 750,000 men lining up against just 300,000. Three quarters of all the German guns on the Western Front – around 6,600 – would be brought in and they would face just slightly more than 2,000 available to the British. As well as numerical superiority in men and firepower, Ludendorff believed he had tactical advantages too. He divided his divisions into shock troops or stormtroopers, attack troops and follow-up groups. The old method of attack – advancing lines of men – was not to be used. Instead, his troops would break through wherever it was possible, penetrating deep into British lines without waiting for support from the flanks. Follow-up units would then move in to clear up the area that had been taken and consolidate it.

The offensive would begin with a brief but intense bombardment, its brevity intended to allow the German troops to take the British unawares. Initial bombardment was targeted at the British rear, aimed at putting command centres out of action and disrupting communication with the front line. It was also hoped that it would disable some of the enemy artillery. With that achieved, the guns would then be turned on the enemy's front.

But, the age-old problem would then be encountered. As the troops moved forward, the guns would be rendered useless, being too far behind the advancing force. It would, therefore, be up to the stormtroopers to take advantage of their position without the support of artillery. It could be a recipe for disaster.

Meanwhile, Ludendorff had not entirely denuded the Eastern Front of German troops or ambition. In fact, there were around fifty divisions, a million men, still stationed there. As has already been noted, when the Bolsheviks broke off negotiations with the Germans, Ludendorff ordered his men to resume their advance on Petrograd. Indeed, the Germans had expansionist objectives in the east and they had set their sights on parts of European Russia. On 3 March, the Treaty of Brest-Litovsk was finally signed, the Russians agreeing to some pretty draconian conditions. They were forced to renounce their claims on Finland, Ukraine, Lithuania, Courland, Livonia and Poland, representing 30 per cent of the country's population as well as 90 per cent of its coal reserves and 50 per cent of its industry. The German divisions in the east were kept there to ensure that the terms of the treaty were fulfilled and they were soon needed in Ukraine where the German puppet regime collapsed within a week. Crimea was also occupied and German troops advanced on the Baku oilfields in the Caucasus. The initiative to secure the oilfields for Germany continued even as the war was finally being lost in the west.

Ludendorff's actions in this sphere are open to severe criticism. It can only be imagined the impact half a million troops would have had on the Western Front had the German High Command been prepared to renounce its ambitions in the east.

Ludendorff's Spring Offensives

The first German offensive of 1918 was named Operation Michael, although it is sometimes known as *Kaiserschlacht* (the Kaiser's Battle). It was launched on 21 March on the old Somme battlefields where German stormtroopers, armed with light machine guns and flamethrowers, advanced towards the British Third and Fifth Armies behind a creeping barrage and a heavy smoke screen. They were using infiltration tactics known as 'Hutier tactics', after General Oskar von Hutier who devised them. The British held their line in the north but in the south they were forced back towards Amiens. In the first week the German troops in the south advanced 40 miles across a front 50 miles wide, coming close to cutting the link between the British and French positions and threatening the vital rail junction of Amiens. With reserves being rushed up to the front by the Allies, the Germans got to within 62 miles of Paris itself, putting the city within range of their artillery. Three heavy Krupp railway guns fired 183 shells on the capital, forcing many Parisians to flee the city. In fact, the offensive was so successful that a jubilant Kaiser Wilhelm declared 24 March a national holiday. It appeared that victory was within reach.

With the situation deteriorating, the Allies hastily summoned a meeting of the Supreme War Council at Doullens where the French Marshal Foch was appointed commander-in-chief of all the Allied armies, with Haig and Pétain reporting to him. But, the Germans were by this time nearing exhaustion, their supply lines overextended and their artillery yet to catch up with them. The British, meanwhile, were using trains to rush to the front reserves and guns from the French sector as well as from the section of the British front the Germans had not attacked and from Britain itself.

Foch succeeded in bringing the German offensive to a standstill. The failure of the assault proved particularly damaging to German morale. German troops had been told that the Allies were suffering similar food shortages to them but, when they overran British positions, they found supplies in abundance, proving this was not the case. Operation Michael ended with 270,000 German and around 240,000 Allied casualties.

Ludendorff was not yet finished, however. Swinging his force north, he launched another offensive, Operation Georgette. On 9 April German troops attacked in an area south of the Ypres Salient with the objective of cutting off the Channel ports of Calais, Boulogne and Dunkirk. These were desperate moments for the British, leading Haig to issue a famous order of the day on 11 April:

'There is no other course open to us but to fight it out! Every position must be held to the last man; there must be no retirement. With our backs to the wall and believing in the justice of our cause, each one of us must fight on to the end.'

Once again, Ludendorff enjoyed initial success, particularly against a couple of Portuguese divisions his troops encountered. The precious ground gained by the Allies at huge cost at Passchendaele the previous year was given up and ferocious fighting took place around Mount Kemmel. Towards the end of April, British reinforcements arrived and Ludendorff brought the offensive to an end. As ever, the casualty numbers were staggering. There were 76,000 British casualties, 35,000 French, 6,000 Portuguese and 109,000 German.

Despite failure and the heavy losses incurred, the relentless Ludendorff planned a third offensive, Operation Blücher, this time along the Aisne river. His target was the French whom he decided to attack on the Chemin des Dames. It began on 27 May and again delivered immediate results. For some reason the French commander, General Denis Duchêne (1862–1950), positioned almost all of his force in the forward zone, making it easy for German gunners to pick them off. In another part of this front was a British force that had been sent there to recover after Operation Michael. The Germans advanced 40 miles in the first three days of the offensive and Paris was once again within reach. As French reserves arrived, however, the German advance slowed, but Ludendorff now made the capital, a mere 40 miles away, his objective. He rushed in reserves from Flanders but, by the time they arrived, it was too late. The French had consolidated their positions and Ludendorff's troops were unable to regain their momentum. Meanwhile, the casualty numbers continued to grow.

The Americans were now in the area and Ludendorff realised that speed was of the essence. This meant that the next two offensives he launched were done without any preparation or proper planning, fatal in such circumstances. He attacked north of the Chemin des Dames on 9 June and on the River Marne on 15 July. As well as being poorly planned, these offensives also lacked the element of surprise and the Allies were ready for them, bringing them to a standstill with artillery and the introduction of reserves.

The German efforts between March and July had been staggering. They had captured significant amounts of ground – more, in fact than had been taken by Allied forces in three years of war. But the territory they had gained really gave them nothing. It was of little strategic importance and they had failed to take the important rail hubs of Amiens and Hazebrouck. The tactics Ludendorff had employed also led to there being large bulges in the German front line, resulting in a larger line to be defended than before. His troops, consequently, were more thinly spread along its length. Worst of all, he had lost around a million men, the Allies about 100,000 fewer. This was disastrous for German prospects in the war, lacking the almost limitless supply of troops that the Allies now enjoyed with the addition of the Americans to their side.

Ludendorff next tried to take advantage of the fact that French reserves had been brought south from Flanders, planning a new offensive there where the British had been left holding the line. His plans would come to nothing, however, because as he arrived in Flanders, the Allies were themselves preparing to go on the offensive.

The Hundred Days Offensive

On 18 July, the Allies, in the form of the French Tenth and Sixth Armies, supported by 750 tanks, attacked the flank of the large salient that Ludendorff's troops had created in the fighting of the previous two months. Massively outnumbered, and with inadequately prepared troops, the Germans retreated. Soon the Allies were attacking both flanks of the salient, forcing the enemy even further back. By the end of the first week of August the Germans were once again back at the Aisne. Ludendorff understandably abandoned his offensive in Flanders, concentrating purely on defending his positions to the south. As usual, the French advance halted, the troops exhausted, supply lines over-extended and the Germans having stabilised their positions. With the situation once again complete stalemate, it was up to the British to carry the day. An offensive was planned by the British Fourth Army to the south of the Somme, the objective being to eliminate the threat of German long-range artillery to the rail hub at Amiens. It did not look auspicious in some respects. The British had lost huge quantities of weaponry in the first six months of 1918 – more than 1,000 artillery pieces, for example, had gone. Manpower too, had suffered and a division in Haig's army now amounted to around half the number of men that it had two years previously. In one area, however, the British were vastly superior. The British munitions industry had performed miracles in re-supplying the army and this was bolstered by the prodigious quantities of Lewis guns, machine guns, trench mortars, gas and shells that were arriving daily, not to mention the much improved tanks rolling out of the factories. Therefore, the British were able to be even more effective with fewer troops, having a great deal more firepower available to them, and it was firepower, above all, that mattered at this stage of the war, rather than the number of men that could be sent into battle.

The Germans, on the other hand, were in a parlous position. Industrial output had plummeted, and the extremely effective British blockade had deprived factories of vital raw materials necessary for the manufacture of munitions. Furthermore, the military had, since August 1916, been in control of just about every aspect of the German economy and their management of the sectors of industry producing munitions and weapons had been little short of catastrophic. For example, they had ordered a huge programme of factory-construction, but there was not enough steel to make the shells. They also neglected the railways, failing to maintain and upgrade where necessary, making it difficult to transport much-needed war materials. Meanwhile, there were still desperate food shortages in Germany, again often as a result of mismanagement by the military. This led to a great deal of unrest, a fall in wages, strikes and severe hunger, all of which contributed significantly to the fall in production. The war, therefore, was developing into an unequal struggle. The Germans were no longer able to supply the weaponry needed to replace what had been captured or destroyed by the Allies.

On 8 August, the Allies launched what became known as the Hundred Days Offensive near Amiens. The American Expeditionary Force, under the command of General John J Pershing (1860–1948), had now arrived in France and it gave renewed impetus to the Allies. The British Army had also been reinforced by a large number of troops that had arrived from campaigns in Palestine and Italy and troops that had been held in reserve in Britain were also now on French soil. The Allies attacked with more than 500 tanks and 120,000 British, Dominion and French troops and by the end of that first day had achieved almost unparallelled success. They had advanced eight miles, killed or wounded 27,000 enemy troops and captured 400 German guns, all for the loss of only 6,500 men. They took the enemy completely by surprise, the British Fourth Army breaking through the German lines and tanks being used to attack rear positions. A 15-mile-long gap had been punched in the German lines south of the Somme and the morale of the German troops fell even further. Ludendorff would later describe this day as the 'Black Day of the German army'. The Allies advanced 14 miles before stiff German resistance stopped them on 12 August.

The British success can be ascribed, mostly, to its artillery. At the Battle of Amiens they were able to employ twice the number of guns available to the Germans. Sound-ranging was now a sophisticated science and the British could accurately pinpoint enemy weaponry, enabling them to surprise the enemy and also to wipe out their batteries. The tactic of the creeping barrage also facilitated the British advance, forcing German machine gunners to keep their heads down until the arrival of the advancing troops approaching behind the barrage, using mortars, Lewis guns and rifle-grenades to good effect. The tank, now in the far more effective Mark V version, also finally came into its own.

On 15 August, Foch demanded that Haig persevere with the Amiens offensive, even though his troops were by this time exhausted and were beginning to outrun their supply line and supporting artillery. Haig refused, preparing instead a fresh offensive by the British Third Army at Albert. Allied commanders seem to have learned by this time that it was futile to persevere with an offensive once the enemy had re-grouped. It was also pointless and costly to advance far beyond the supply line and supporting artillery. Therefore, rather than waste more lives as would have happened in the past, Haig decided to turn his attention elsewhere, making brief attacks which were stopped once the initial forward momentum was lost. The end of an offensive on one part of the front was greeted by the start of a fresh one on another part of the line. The Germans were constantly wrong-footed.

The next phase of the campaign was launched with the Battle of Albert, starting on 21 August. During the last week of August the pressure exerted by the Allies on the German lines along the front was unrelenting. After capturing Albert on 22 August, they pushed the Germans back over a 34-mile front. In the south, on 17 August, the French Tenth Army began the Second Battle of Noyon, taking the town 12 days later. To the north of the initial attack, on 26 August the British First Army fought the Second Battle of Arras of the year. After fierce fighting, Bapaume fell on 29 August to New Zealand troops who had to fight through the exceptionally well-fortified Le Transloy-Loupart trench system. In four weeks of fighting, the Allies had taken more than 100,000 German prisoners and at last it was time for even Ludendorff to realise that all was lost. 'We cannot win the war anymore,' he said, 'but we must not lose it either.' Eventually, on 2 September, in the face of such pressure, German High Command ordered a withdrawal to the Hindenburg Line in the south. The scene was set for the culmination of the conflict in a series of battles in the autumn.

Foch now launched what is sometimes called the 'Grand Offensive' with 50 divisions of British troops, supported by Belgians in the north and large numbers of French and Americans in the south widening the battle until it covered virtually the entire Western Front. On 26 September the offensive began with 22 divisions of French and 15 divisions of American troops attacking in the Meuse-Argonne area. The Americans had so far played only a supporting role in the war, helping the French on the Marne in mid 1918 and the Australians at Hamel in July. They had also been involved in clearing the St Mihiel Salient, south of Verdun, on 12 September. This, therefore, was their first major action and their inexperience showed, especially in the face of the strong defences that the Germans had built in the area and difficult terrain that made it impossible for tanks to be used. By October, they had gained only 15 miles but finally on 17 October they broke through the Hindenburg Line. Their advance had been inexorably slow but it had at least occupied 36 enemy divisions in the area which was very helpful to the other Allied armies.

Operations in the north were launched on 27 September when five British and two French armies, the Belgian army and a couple of divisions of American troops that were serving with the British attacked the Hindenburg Line. The objective was to punch a hole in the formidable defences that were occasionally three miles deep, with copious amounts of barbed wire and regular concrete machine gun posts. The principal point of difficulty was the St

Quentin Canal with its steep banks and muddy water six feet deep in places. Tanks were obviously of no use there but the canal would also prove a very difficult obstacle for infantry. At one point to the north it flowed through a tunnel which, although it would make the going easier, was heavily defended. It was decided to go back to the old methods and unleash a long and intense bombardment on the line in order to destroy as much of the German defences as possible. Of great help to the Allies were some captured plans of a part of these defences that disclosed the whereabouts of every machine gun post, artillery emplacement and trench. They had also been supplied with enormous quantities of high explosive shells and planned to repeat the success they had enjoyed at Amiens with them. On 29 September the barrage began and before long the German guns had been silenced. The British Fourth Army led by Australian troops attacked the canal while the French First Army assaulted fortifications outside the town of St Quentin. On the canal in the northern sector, the German defences held and the advance across the tunnel was stalled. In the south, however, the British made their way across, breaching the Hindenburg Line on a three-mile front. The Germans were now outflanked and the troops held up at the tunnel were able to proceed. By 5 October, the Allies had penetrated the Hindenburg Line along a 19-mile front. The state of the German army at the time is summed up by General Sir Henry Rawlinson:

'Had the Boche [Germans] not shown marked signs of deterioration during the past month, I should never have contemplated attacking the Hindenburg Line. Had it been defended by the Germans of two years ago, it would certainly have been impregnable… '

The statistics of the bombardment are astonishing. During every minute of the attack 126 shells from field guns alone fell on every 500 yards of the German defences, an onslaught that continued for eight hours. Now Allied commanders no longer believed that the war would be ended by a massive attack in 1919, as had been thought. They realised it was there for the winning in the autumn of 1918.

Throughout October and into November, the Germans retreated through the territories they had seized in 1914 in the very first months of the war, the Allies harrying them with a series of steady offensives, pushing them still further back. The Germans were disorganised and dispensed with heavy equipment and supplies as they retreated, further damaging their already low morale and rendering it impossible for them to resist attacks. There were rearguard actions, however, with heavy casualties on both sides – the Battle of Courtrai on 14 October; the Battle of Mont-D'Origny the following day; the Battle of Lys and Escaut on 20 October; the Battle of the Serre the same day; the Battle of Valenciennes on 1 November and the Battle of the Sambre, the Battle of Guise and the Battle of Thiérache on 4 November.

On 28 September Ludendorff, close to mental breakdown and often in tears, had recommended to the Kaiser that peace should be sought. He then changed his mind, believing that the German army should hold out until winter set in, making it easier to defend their positions. In Germany, however, the new civilian government that had been appointed under the leadership of Prince Maximilian of Baden (1867–1929) chose to ignore Ludendorff's plan and instead worked to initiate peace negotiations. Eventually, on 26 October, Ludendorff was dismissed by the Kaiser. The situation was, indeed, desperate. The German army was devastated, having lost 6 million men, the country was riven with strikes, and there was a mutiny in the navy. Revolution appeared to be a very real prospect.

On the night of 7–8 November, a German delegation crossed the French lines and opened negotiations with the Allies. They gathered with their Allied counterparts in a railway carriage in a forest near the town of Compiègne. Representing the Allies were Marshal Foch, his right-hand man General Maxime Weygand (1867–1965), First Sea Lord Admiral Rosslyn Wemyss (1864–1933), and Deputy First Sea Lord Admiral George Hope (1869–1959). From the German side there were the politician Matthias Erzberger (1875–1921), Count Alfred von Oberndorff (1870–1963) from the German Foreign Ministry, Major General Detlof von Winterfeldt (1867–1940) from the German army and Captain Ernst Vanselow from the navy. There was no question of negotiation and the Germans had little option but to accept what the Allies put in front of them. The Armistice demanded an end to hostilities; complete German demilitarisation; the evacuation of all German troops from France, Belgium, Alsace-Lorraine and Luxembourg within 14 days; removal of German troops from territory on the west side of the Rhine with 19-mile radius bridgeheads on the right side of the river at Mainz, Koblenz and Cologne as well as occupation by Allied forces; evacuation of all German troops from the Eastern Front; renunciation of the Treaty of Brest-Litovsk with Russia and the Treaty of Bucharest with Romania; the internment of the German High Seas Fleet; the surrender of all German U-boats, and cannons, machine guns, mortars, planes, locomotives and railway carriages.

The Germans had initially tried to negotiate with United States President Wilson, believing that he would not be as harsh as the British but Wilson demanded the abdication of the Kaiser. In fact, the Kaiser, horrified by events recognised that he would have to give up the German crown but hoped to retain the throne of Prussia. This turned out to be a forlorn hope and on 9 November, without any fuss, the Social Democrat Philipp Scheidemann (1865–1939) declared that Germany was a republic. The Weimar Republic was born. Wilhelm, meanwhile, went into exile in the Netherlands.

Although the news of the Armistice was given to the troops on the morning of 11 November, there was still intense fighting until the very last minute before 11 am, the time given for an end to hostilities. Many British artillery units, for instance, were reluctant to carry away their heavy spare ammunition. Therefore, they continued firing on German positions. The Allies were also making the most of their superiority, ensuring that, in the event of hostilities being resumed, they were in the best position possible. This explains how on the final day of the war, there were 10,944 casualties, of whom 2,738 died. One battery of the US Navy unleashed its last shell at 10.57 am, timed to land far behind the German lines just before 11 am.

The last Frenchman to die was Augustin Trébuchon (1878–1918) who was on his way to inform his colleagues that hot soup would be served after the ceasefire when he was shot; the last British soldier to fall was George Edwin Ellison (1878–1918) who was killed that morning on the outskirts of Mons in Belgium, just ninety minutes before the end of the war. The last soldier to die in the First World War is recognised to be the American Henry Gunther (1895–1918), killed just sixty seconds before the Armistice came into force while charging confused German troops who were fully aware that the end of the war was imminent.

Finally, at 11 o'clock in the morning of 11 November, the war on the Western Front ended.

Collapse on the Eastern Front

Nothing much had happened in the Balkans since 1915 but in September 1918 there was finally some activity. British, French and Serbian forces, under the command of the much respected General Louis Franchet d'Esperey (1856–1942), and with a great deal of heavy artillery, moved into action against Bulgaria from Salonika. Given what was happening elsewhere, there was little chance that Bulgaria would receive any help from her Central Powers allies and her forces were soon in serious trouble. The Serbs broke through at the Battle of Vardar and after that the entire front was overrun. The Bulgarian government sued for peace and by the end of September an armistice had been declared. A number of German commanders claimed after the war that it was Bulgaria's collapse that forced them to seek peace, but it is probably more the case that small countries like Bulgaria lost their stomach for the fight the moment it became obvious that Germany was going to lose the war. However, it was critical as Germany now lost its main supplies of oil and food.

The end on the Italian front had been coming for a while. On 15 June, bolstered by reinforcements introduced after the end of the fighting against Russia, the Austro-Hungarians launched the offensive that became known as the Battle of the Piave River along which Cadorna's replacement, General Diaz, had established strong defences. In charge of the Hapsburg troops was the new Austrian Chief-of-Staff, Arthur Arz von Straussenburg (1857–1935) who was tasked with finishing off the Italians after the disaster of Caporetto. Ludendorff was supportive of an offensive as he hoped that it would force the Allies to divert some of the newly arrived American troops from the Western Front. But the offensive was a disaster for the Austro-Hungarians, finally ordered to retreat on 20 June by Emperor Karl – Franz Joseph had died in 1916 – who had personally taken command. At one point in the battle, an estimated 20,000 of his troops drowned while trying to reach the east bank of the swollen Piave and in total 60,000 died in the battle.

The Hapsburg army was now in such a dreadful state that it could no longer fight. There was no food, and transport and equipment were also in very short supply. Around 20,000 deserted and by the end of the month another 20,000 had followed them back home. On 24 October, the Italians successfully launched their offensive against a ghost of an army in the Battle of Vittorio Veneto and not long after it was all over. By that time the map of the world was changing. On 28 October, the Czecho-Slovaks had proclaimed a new state in Prague; the following day, the South Slavs – Slovenes, Croats and Serbs – proclaimed independence; and on 31 October, the Empire of Austria-Hungary was consigned to history when Hungary withdrew from the union and ordered its troops home.

On 28 October, Austria's military leaders ordered a general retreat but the Italians kept advancing, taking Trieste on 3 November. In this advance and retreat, Austria-Hungary incurred around 30,000 casualties and around half a million men were taken prisoner while the Italians lost 37,461 dead and wounded. The Austrians had sued for peace on 29 October and it was signed on 3 November, becoming effective twenty-four hours later. But, the Italians continued to advance until 3 pm on 4 November, occupying all of the Tyrol, including the town of Innsbruck.

The Austrian-Italian Armistice of Villa Giusti stipulated that Austria-Hungary's troops should evacuate all of the territory they had captured since 1914 as well as South Tyrol, Tarvisio, the Isonzo

Valley, Gorizia, Trieste, Istria, Western Carniola and Dalmatia; German forces were to leave Austria-Hungary and the Allies were to have free use of Austria-Hungary's communications, enabling them to reach Germany from the south.

7

Peace at a Price

In Flanders fields the poppies blow
Between the crosses, row on row,
That mark our place; and in the sky
The larks, still bravely singing, fly
Scarce heard amid the guns below.
From 'In Flanders Fields' by John McCrae

Any peace settlement at the end of the war had to achieve several things. Firstly, of course, there was the matter of revenge. France and Belgium had suffered greatly and although they desired revenge for the wrongs done to them, they also wanted to have security that it would not happen again. The settlement would have to provide a means of moving on from the horror of the conflict and hopefully to create a new world order, one that would ensure that wars of this magnitude never happened again. Woodrow Wilson was instrumental in the latter, 'Wilsonian idealism' being the term used to describe his views about government and the conduct of the peace. However, even to Wilson, Germany had been entirely in the wrong in starting the war and had, furthermore, fought it in a manner that was contrary to the customs and conventions involved in relations between countries. He was in agreement with the pacifists and radicals on that matter and the settlement would have to deal with it.

Germany, meanwhile, proudly contrived somehow to create a victory out of its defeat. Post-war it was argued that, after all, the German army had not been defeated in the field and when the armistice was declared, her troops still held territory on all fronts. Moreover, its front had not been breached. Therefore, many claimed, it was not a defeat at all. The troops were welcomed back to Berlin by Germany's new Chancellor, Friedrich Ebert (1871–1925), with the words, 'I salute you who return unvanquished from the field of battle'. Those who argued thus claimed – concurring with Ludendorff who in 1917 had been aggrieved at the way that the demoralisation on the home front had begun to seep into the minds of his own troops – that the troops had been stabbed in the back by the revolution in Germany. Nonetheless, the demands presented to Germany's senior delegate to the peace conference in Paris on 7 May 1919 elicited a shocked response. 'Germany renounces its existence,' he said. Indeed, not allowed to participate in the negotiations, the German government issued a formal protest against what it saw as unfair demands. German Foreign Minister Ulrich von Brockdorff-Rantzau told Clemenceau:

'We know the full brunt of hate that confronts us here. You demand from us to confess we were the only guilty party of war; such a confession in my mouth would be a lie.'

Indeed, regarding its exclusion to be a 'violation of honour', Germany withdrew completely from the proceedings.

The conference, key recommendations of which were rolled into the various treaties – Versailles, Saint-Germain-en-Laye, Neuilly-sur-Seine, Trianon, and Sèvres – involved representatives from thirty-seven countries and nationalities. The so-called 'Big Four', President Woodrow Wilson of the United States, British Prime Minister David Lloyd George, Italian Prime Minister Vittorio Orlando (1860–1952) and French Prime Minister

Georges Clemenceau, met together 145 times and, in reality, the major decisions were all taken by them, to be ratified later by the other representatives. Germany lost conquered territories that were occupied by people who were not German, including lands captured in previous conflicts such as Polish territory that had been annexed as far back as the eighteenth century and land captured from Denmark and France in wars between 1864 and 1871. Needless to say, France, Belgium and Russia were divested of German occupation. It was all as stipulated in President Wilson's Fourteen Points. Unlike after the Second World War, however, Germany was not rendered impotent. Its industries were left untouched and its unity and territorial integrity were left intact. The French military had a desire to see the Rhineland turned into a French dependency to ensure France's security but this was denied. In fact, Germany, although defeated, remained the pre-eminent industrial power on the European continent.

It was hoped that by banning her from being able to maintain a large conscript army, Germany would never again be able to wage a similar war in the future. It was also forbidden for her to have battleships, submarines or an air force. German forces could not be stationed on the west bank of the Rhine and most importantly of all in the demilitarisation of the Rhineland, an Allied army of occupation would be stationed there for the next fifteen years. Of course, this left the French government feeling distinctly nervous. What, they argued, would stop a future German government from ignoring the terms of the treaty? And would the Allies have the resolve to take action against Germany if that occurred? Nonetheless, the British and the Americans resisted demands that the Rhineland be taken away from Germany. In order to assuage French fears, Wilson gave a guarantee that an act of aggression by a future German government would be considered an act of war against the United States and Great Britain.

Germany was also required to pay reparations for the damage it had caused, in particular to France and Belgium on whose territory the war in the west had been waged. Many families had, of course, been left without husbands and fathers, but vast swathes of land had also been completely devastated by constant fighting and relentless shelling. As well as land being destroyed by warfare, there had also been deliberate acts of destruction, carried out by both invading and retreating German troops. The Allies – especially France and Belgium – believed that Germany should be held responsible for the re-construction of their lands and the maintenance of families robbed of their principal breadwinner. Article 231 of the Treaty of Versailles declared Germany and her allies to be responsible for all 'loss and damage' suffered by the Allies and detailed the terms for the payment of reparations. In January 1921, the Inter-Allied Reparations Commission set the total amount to be paid at 269 billion gold marks, the equivalent of 100,000 tonnes of pure gold. This was equivalent to about £13 billion. It was a sum that many economists believed to be excessive. The actual total payout between 1921 and 1931, when payments were indefinitely suspended, was 20 billion gold marks, worth about a billion pounds sterling. The rhetoric of 1919 regarding payment for veterans' benefits and all the damages was no more than that – rhetoric – and had little to do with the amount paid. Basically, the sum was based on Germany's ability to pay rather than what was needed to put everything right. Germany's allies, Austria, Hungary and Turkey, were in such a poor state economically, that even though they were supposed to contribute to reparations, in actual fact they paid very little. Adolf Hitler cancelled Germany's reparation payments when he became

Chancellor in 1933 but the London Conference in 1953 required the resumption of the payments and the final installment was paid on 3 October 2010.

The peace conference ended on 21 January 1920 when the inaugural General Assembly of the League of Nations was held. This intergovernmental organisation was listed in Wilson's Fourteen Points and had the simple objective of maintaining world peace. It would do so, according to its Covenant, through collective security and disarmament and by settling international disputes and disagreements through negotiation and arbitration. It would also be vigilant about labour conditions, treatment of native inhabitants, the trafficking of drugs and people, health, prisoners of war and the safeguarding of the interests of minorities in Europe. It was dissolved in 1946 and the greatest number of member nations it had was 58 from September 1934 to February 1935. The League would have no standing army to back up its resolutions and would, instead, depend upon the 'Great Powers' to do so. These were Great Britain, France, Italy, and Japan which were the only nations to occupy permanent seats on the League of Nations Council, the organisation's executive body. Ironically, the United States Senate voted against ratifying the Treaty of Versailles in 1920 which prevented America from becoming a member of the League. There were a number of reasons for this. Some suggested that Wilson's refusal to include prominent Republican politicians in the American delegation to the peace talks had antagonised that party and certainly a number of Republicans in the US Senate – known as the 'Irreconcilables' – opposed the treaty. They wanted a treaty with some reservations, especially with reference to Article X that gave the League the power to declare war without a vote by the US Congress. Many in America – particularly those of German and Irish descent – denounced the treaty because, they claimed, it favoured the British. When President Wilson was succeeded by the Republican Warren G Harding, the new president continued the opposition to the Treaty and the League, passing the Knox-Porter Resolution on 21 July 1921 that formally brought an end to hostilities between the United States and the Central Powers. The United States finally signed peace treaties with Germany, Austria and Hungary in August 1921.

In Germany, resentment of the treaty persisted. It was known as the 'Diktat', as its terms were presented to the government without any opportunity for response. The country's first democratically elected Chancellor, Philipp Scheidemann, resigned rather than sign the treaty, declaring it to be 'unacceptable'. A new coalition emerged, headed by Gustav Bauer (1870–1944). However, it was obvious that Germany had little choice but to sign. President Ebert asked Hindenburg whether the army was in a fit state to put up resistance should hostilities be resumed, because if the treaty remained unsigned by Germany, that was what would inevitably happen. It was quickly made clear to him, however, that such a position was untenable. The treaty was signed on 28 June 1919 but it was still condemned by nationalists, conservatives and Germany's former military leaders. The loyalties of those who supported it – socialists, communists and Jews – were viewed as suspicious and it was suggested, once again, that they had 'stabbed Germany in the back'. This reinforced the view that responsibility for Germany's defeat lay at the feet of those who had instigated strikes in the arms industry just when the Spring Offensive appeared to be bearing fruit. These strikes were said to have been instigated by agitators and Jews were singled out for most of the blame. It was a state of affairs that would be exploited by Adolf Hitler and the Nazi party during their rise to power.

The Political Aftermath

The map of Europe was entirely different after the war. The great empires and imperial dynasties – the Romanovs of Russia, the Hohenzollerns of Germany, the Hapsburgs of Austria-Hungary and the Ottoman Sultans – that had been in power for centuries had disappeared.

The Treaty of Brest-Litovsk was rendered invalid by the Allies at the end of the war. It had allowed for Germany and Austria-Hungary to determine 'in accordance with their populations' the futures of Estonia, Finland, Latvia, Lithuania and the Congress of Poland. This meant that the status of a great deal of Eastern Europe remained uncertain after the war. There were great changes, however. After more than a century of Russian hegemony, Poland was once again an independent nation. One of the terms of the Treaty of Versailles saw Germany obliged to give small amounts of territory to Denmark, Czechoslovakia, Belgium and much more to France. The largest tract of land she was forced to cede, however, was to form part of the new Poland. This land included the German port of Danzig and the corridor it created separated East Prussia from the rest of Germany. This caused outrage in Germany, a sentiment upon which the Nazis would seize to emphasise the unfairness, to their minds at least, of Germany's treatment in the treaties.

In the regions of Austria-Hungary, radical nationalism took hold in many places, even before the Armistice. Central government had ceased to operate in a number of territories and groups formed to try to fill the void this created. They tried to establish governments in the name of various political ideals and of different nationalities. The treaties had stipulated that Allied forces should occupy the Austro-Hungarian Empire to maintain stability, but that would have taken many more troops than were now available to them. It was a hugely complicated situation, as nationalists who had helped the Allies during the war now turned to them for self-determination. The Fourteen Points stated that nationalities should be allowed to decide their own future and government. This brought a concern from the French who were worried by the security threat that an even larger Germany would represent. The treaties, therefore, upset the ambitions of a great many and instead of the peace and stability that had been spoken of and an end to the quarrelling of the past fifty years, the result was more of the same or even worse than what had gone before.

The Republic of German-Austria was created from the German-speaking part of the Hapsburg Empire. It included almost all of the territory of present-day Austria, plus South Tyrol and the town of Tarvisio which are both now part of Italy; southern Carinthia and southern Styria, now Slovenia; and Sudetenland and German Bohemia which are now part of the Czech Republic. It lost a number of other lands where Germans were in the majority. The newly independent Hungary did not include about two-thirds of the lands of the former Kingdom of Hungary. This included large areas where the ethnic Magyars were in a majority. Bohemia, Moravia, Opava Silesia and the western part of the Duchy of Cieszyn, Slovakia and Carpathian Ruthenia were incorporated in the new Czechoslovakia while Galicia, the eastern section of the Duchy of Cieszyn, the northern County of Orava and northern Spisz were transferred to the new Poland. Italy gained the southern half of the County of Tyrol and Trieste. The Kingdom of Serbia was the basis for a new multinational state that included Serbs, Bosnians, Croats and Slovenes. Initially known as the Kingdom of Serbs, Croats and Slovenes, in 1929 it was re-named Yugoslavia. The new nation of Czechoslovakia was created by combining the

Kingdom of Bohemia with parts of the Kingdom of Hungary. Romania gained Transylvania and Bukovina. Russia, now the Union of Soviet Socialist Republics, or the Soviet Union, lost Finland, Estonia, Lithuania and Latvia which all became independent nations. They would only remain thus until 1940 when they were occupied by the Soviet Union.

The problem was that many of the new nations had large national minorities, including millions of Germans who now found themselves in these countries as minorities. These minorities' interests were very often ignored by the new national governments attempting to forge a national identity for their newly created nations. Most of these states started out as democracies, but one by one after the war they descended into some kind of autocratic rule. They quarrelled constantly amongst themselves but remained too weak to be able to compete with any assurance. Thus, when Nazi Germany re-armed and attacked them, the new states of south-central Europe were unable to defend themselves effectively.

Meanwhile, for the nations of Britain's Empire, which were fighting in a major conflict for the first time, the First World War represented a sort of 'coming-of-age'. There was a new pride in their achievements in the war and a new spirit of camaraderie. For Australia and New Zealand, especially, Gallipoli was a defining moment in their nationhood. Canada, too, enjoyed a new feeling of nationhood after fighting alongside the 'mother countries' at battles such as Vimy Ridge, the first time that Canadian divisions fought together as a single corps. For them, it felt like the first occasion on which they had received international respect. The war also began the process of separation of the dominions from the empire. They were automatically obliged to fight by Britain's declaration of war in August 1914, but at the end of the war, they were individual signatories to the Treaty of Versailles.

The modern problems of the Middle East, particularly those of the ongoing disagreements between Palestine and Israel, had their roots in the First World War. Before the outbreak of war, the Ottoman Empire had succeeded in maintaining peace and stability throughout the region but the demise of that empire led to a vacuum and conflicts over claims to territory and nationhood. Frontiers were imposed and nations created by the western powers, often with little thought for the wishes and aspirations of the local populations. Indeed, the new borders often failed to correspond to actual sectarian, tribal or ethnic distinctions. Britain became the dominant power in the region, occupying the territory that would become Iraq, Palestine, Trans-Jordan, Syria and Lebanon but many were unhappy. The Hashemite Arabs were given substantial amounts of territory, but when the British did not fulfil their promises of independence, Arab politics became focused on nationalism and ejecting the colonial powers and their ruling systems. The result, ultimately, was a series of militarist governments that dominated many Arab nations from the 1950s until the Arab Spring of 2011.

The Cost of the War

Of course, there are figures and statistics – more often than not staggering in their size and number – but the cost of the war goes far beyond the numbers of dead and sums of money expended. The human cost blighted Europe for many years to come. Families were devastated and men returned from the horrors of the front blind, having lost limbs or with minds permanently damaged by their experiences. British soldiers who had survived were awarded the War Medal and Victory Medal. A bronze memorial plaque inscribed with the words 'Died for Freedom and Honour' was given to families who had lost a loved one. The rewards for those who had led so many men to their slaughter were greater. Field Marshal Douglas Haig was given an earldom, becoming Earl Haig of Bemersyde, but it did not arrive without some controversy. He was first offered a viscountcy but viewed it as a snub by Lloyd George since Sir John French had been awarded that rank upon his forced resignation. However, he also used the opportunity to bargain for better state financial help for returning soldiers. Lloyd George eventually backed down in March 1919 and Haig received his earldom. He also received the thanks of both Houses of Parliament and a grant of £100,000 – he had requested £250,000 – to allow him to live in the manner befitting a senior peer. Other generals who had been prominent in the war, such as Rawlinson, Gough, Hamilton and Townshend, received knighthoods.

In all, of the 68 million men mobilised by the two sides in the war, 10 million died in battle and a further 21 million were wounded. On average, 5,059 men died every day. Interestingly, the Allies lost 52 per cent of the men they mobilised and the Central Powers 49 per cent. Germany lost 15.1 per cent of its active male population; Austria-Hungary 17.1 per cent; and France lost 10.5 per cent. By 1922, it is estimated that there were between 4.5 million and 7 million homeless children in Russia as a result of the years of war.

However, the loss of life was not restricted to the battlefield. Almost 9 million civilians also died as a result of the war, from starvation and disease as well as in massacres or as a result of genocide, or simply in the course of the fighting. The Spanish Flu pandemic that raged across the world in 1918 and 1919, killing eight million people can also be partly ascribed to the war. It is believed that the close proximity in which people lived as well as massive movements of troops increased the transmission of the disease and facilitated its mutation. It is thought that soldiers' immune systems, weakened by malnourishment and the stress of combat probably increased their susceptibility to the disease. In fact, some commentators suggest that the balance of the war may have been tipped in the Allies' favour as in the last few months of fighting, the illness struck troops of the Central Powers before it hit the Allies.

Land was also a victim of the conflict. In France, 4.9 million acres of farming land and 1.2 million acres of forest were devastated while 3 million houses and buildings were destroyed. This contributed to the actual financial cost of the war which – in 1914–18 terms – has been estimated at almost $126 billion for the Allies and $60.6 billion for the Central Powers. Britain, France and Italy had borrowed substantial amounts of money, mostly from the United States. Of course, the conclusion of the war meant that these debts were now due to be paid. In order to do this rates of personal taxation in Europe rose substantially, in Britain from 9 to 27 per cent and in France from 13 to 18 per cent. They also rose in Germany, from 8 to 12 per cent and even the United States put up personal taxes, from 2 to 8 per cent. The gold reserves of all the combatant nations were, of course, depleted and this was particularly advantageous for America as well as the neutral countries which had not participated in the war.

The collective trauma shared around the world by those affected by the war produced varying reactions. Some, disgusted by the horrors they claimed nationalism had brought to humankind, threw their support behind the League of Nations, hoping for a more internationalist world. Understandably, many embraced pacifism. On the other hand, there were many, their views hardened by the horrors of the war, who believed that only military strength could save the world from a repeat of the recent conflict. Certainly the peace, prosperity and stability of Victorian Britain and the optimism of France's *Belle Epoque* were things of the past. People mourned for years after the war had ended, commemorating the 'Lost Generation' of war dead in thousands of memorials in towns and villages.

In America, Wilson's intervention in the war became extremely unpopular, as shown by the fact that the Versailles Treaty was never ratified by the United States and the country, consequently, never became a member of the League of Nations. This concern about America's involvement in a European war led to the passing of laws in Congress that ensured America's neutrality in the event of another conflict in the future.

In Germany, the 'stab in the back' legend – *Dolchstosslegende* – gained currency after 1918. It held that Germany did not, in fact, lose the war but was betrayed by civilians at home and the republicans who had forced Wilhelm II to abdicate and replaced the monarchy with the Weimar Republic. One of the principal proponents of *Dolchstosslegende* was none other than Erich Ludendorff who became a prominent exponent of right-wing views during the 1920s. The Nazis exploited this view of history during their rise to power. The politicians who signed the armistice were dubbed the 'November Criminals' – *Novemberverbrecher* – and the German people came to see themselves as victims. The Weimar government was discredited, leaving the country destabilised and prey to extreme political movements, both of the left and the right. The German people also resented the harsh conditions imposed upon them by the Treaty of Versailles. Adolf Hitler promised to 'undo this treaty and restore Germany to its old greatness'. Thus, can it be argued that the harsh terms imposed at

Versailles led directly to the Second World War, making a lie of the notion that the First World War was 'a war to end all wars'. As Marshal Ferdinand Foch said after the signing of the Treaty of Versailles:

'This is not a peace. It is an armistice for twenty years.'

Further Reading

There are, of course, countless books about the First World War. Here is a small selection:

Clark, Christopher, *The Sleepwalkers: How Europe Went to War in 1914*, London: Penguin, 2013

Gilbert, Martin, *The First World War*, London: Phoenix, 2008 (first published in 1994)

Hart, Peter, *The Great War*, London: Profile Books, 2014

Keegan, John, *The First World War*, London: Pimlico, 1999

Stevenson, David, *1914–1918: The History of the First World War*, London: Penguin, 2012

Strachan, Hew, *The First World War: A New History*, London: Simon & Schuster, 2014

Walter, George (ed), *The Penguin Book of First World War Poetry*, London: Penguin Classics, 2006

Index